"I AM NOT HAPPY THAT I AM SICK. I AM NOT HAPPY THAT I HAVE AIDS, BUT IF THAT IS HELPING OTHERS, I CAN, AT LEAST, KNOW THAT MY OWN MISFORTUNE HAS HAD SOME POSITIVE WORTH."

This is the story of the man who made that statement just before his death.

He was born Roy Harold Scherer, Jr., but was given the name Rock Hudson by an agent who wanted to build up an image of rugged outdoor masculine strength.

He became one of the most celebrated actors of our time, but his most demanding role was the one he was forced to live for the public that adored him.

He was the hero of many dramas—but never was he more heroic than in his own personal tragedy.

Rock Hudson—ahe screen, and as h in real life. . . .

MARK BEGO, former editor-in-chief of *Modern Screen*, has used his extraordinary knowledge of behind-the-screen Hollywood to tell Rock Hudson's story from beginning to end. Mr. Bego is the author of bestselling biographies of Madonna and Michael Jackson, the latter with two million copies in print.

ROCK HUDSON

PUBLIC AND PRIVATE

AN UNAUTHORIZED BIOGRAPHY

★ MARK BEGO ★

A SIGNET BOOK

NEW AMERICAN LIBRARY

NAL BOOKS ARE AVAILABLE AT QUANTITY DISCOUNTS WHEN
USED TO PROMOTE PRODUCTS OR SERVICES. FOR INFOR-
MATION PLEASE WRITE TO PREMIUM MARKETING DIVISION,
NEW AMERICAN LIBRARY, 1633 BROADWAY, NEW YORK,
NEW YORK 10019.

SIGNET TRADEMARK REG. U.S. PAT. OFF. AND FOREIGN COUNTRIES
REGISTERED TRADEMARK—MARCA REGISTRADA
HECHO EN CHICAGO, U.S.A.

SIGNET, SIGNET CLASSIC, MENTOR, PLUME, MERIDIAN AND NAL BOOKS
are published by New American Library,
1633 Broadway, New York, New York 10019

First Printing, April, 1986

1 2 3 4 5 6 7 8 9

PRINTED IN THE UNITED STATES OF AMERICA

This book is dedicated to the men and women around the world who are working this very minute to find a cure for AIDS.

The author would like to thank the following people for helping to research, compile, and verify much of the information contained in this book:

Bart Andrews   Toni Lopopolo
Joe Canole   Susan Mittelkauf
Jaine Fabian   Marie Morreale
Farley Granger   Kevin Mulroy
Charles Hunt   Jim Pinkston
Randy Jones   Sherry Robb
Barb & Jeff Knudsen David Salidor
Phillip LaCasia   Matt Sartwell
Mark Lasswell   Kelly West

and all of the "confidential" sources, quoted herein, whose names do not appear in this book.

CONTENTS

INTRODUCTION

FOR MORE than thirty years Rock Hudson embodied the personable, handsome, and virile movie star. His six-foot, four-inch frame, his clean-cut all-American good looks, and his appealing manner made him one of the most idolized stars of the century. But throughout his career, he carried with him a secret about his private life.

Rock Hudson hit the pinnacle of his film career in 1956, when he starred opposite Elizabeth Taylor in *Giant*, a role that established his reputation as a pillar of masculine power and that would earn him a "Best Actor" Oscar nomination. His subsequent teaming with Doris Day for three pictures in the late 1950s and early 1960s set a new style in sexy sophistication, and made him the romantic idol of millions of female moviegoers. More than twenty years later, in 1985, Rock Hudson proved that he could still cast his virile spell when he starred opposite Linda Evans in the hit TV series *Dynasty*. That same year the world was stunned by the news that Rock Hudson was gay, and that he was dying of AIDS. His public admission of his homosexuality was selflessly made in an effort to save lives—and to dispel the atmosphere of unspeakable shame and fear the disease has created. In doing so, Rock Hudson became a hero more courageous than any protagonist he ever portrayed on screen. His tragic death has left Hollywood and his millions of fans devastated, but also in awe of his immense talent and personal strength.

Born Roy Harold Scherer, Jr., on November 17, 1925, Rock Hudson fell in love with the idea of becoming a film star when he saw Jon Hall rescuing Dorothy Lamour in a 1937 film called *The Hurricane*. He worked as a navy aircraft mechanic in World War II, and when the war ended, he decided to move to California and attempt to fulfill his dream of breaking into the movies.

Rock was discovered by an agent named Henry Willson. At the time, the young actor was supporting himself by driving a truck. Willson decided to take him under his wing and created a heroic macho image for Roy by giving him a name that would signify power and strength. Borrowing from the Rock of Gibraltar and the Hudson River, Rock Hudson was born.

Making his film debut in the 1948 production of *Fighter Squadron*, Rock Hudson appeared in twenty-six films over the next six years, including adventure dramas like *Undertow* (1949), *One Way Street* (1950), *Winchester '73* (1950), *Desert Hawk* (1950), *Air Cadet* (1951), *Bend in the River* (1952), and *Sea Devils* (1953).

It was in 1954 that Rock's star image gelled when he appeared with Jane Wyman in the remake of *Magnificent Obsession*. It was during this same period that the popular 1950s scandal sheet *Confidential* contacted Rock's studio, announcing that it had conclusive evidence that Rock Hudson was homosexual and that it planned to publish the story. In an effort to keep the allegations of Rock's homosexuality from appearing in print, the studio urged the magazine to run instead a story about a lesser-known gay actor George Nader.

Hastily, a "fixed" marriage for Rock Hudson was

arranged as a publicity ploy by Henry Willson, who hoped that a marriage would forever quell allegations of Hudson's homosexuality. In 1955 Rock eloped with Willson's longtime secretary Phyllis Gates. The marriage lasted less than three years but effectively created a smoke screen around Rock's private life. In 1956 Rock Hudson made the film *Giant,* and suddenly he was a bona-fide superstar and America's top male sex symbol. For the next fifteen years, rumors about his homosexuality were again dismissed as slanderous Hollywood gossip.

In a career move that made him America's top male box-office draw, Rock turned from adventure films and drama to sparkling comedies opposite Doris Day. Day was destined to become linked with him as his most famous leading lady. Their three romantic farces—*Pillow Talk* (1959), *Lover Come Back* (1961), and *Send Me No Flowers* (1964)—defined the moral values and humor of early sixties "New Frontier" America. The films in which Doris Day appeared as the bubbly contemporary career woman and Rock Hudson appeared as the suave, smooth, and sexy bachelor made them the most famous cinema couple of the era.

As the decade changed, so did Rock's screen persona. In a cinematic era of spies and espionage, Hudson portrayed a series of macho adventurers in such films as *Blindfold* (1966), *Seconds* (1966), *Tobruk* (1966), *Ice Station Zebra* (1967), *The Undefeated* (1969), and *Hornet's Nest* (1969). His rugged hero image remained intact as he began his third decade as a screen idol and the dream lover of millions of women.

Even for a dashing forty-five-year-old screen star, however, the opportunities to play romantic leads were dwindling. The late sixties counterculture ushered in a whole new brand of younger leading men like Peter Fonda and Jack Nicholson. Rock found himself in need of a vehicle to revitalize his career, and in 1971, starring in the hit television show *McMillan and Wife*, he found one. The successful show put Rock into millions of households each week. The series drew fantastic ratings and ran through 1977. Rock and costar Susan Saint James played a clever and amusing crime-fighting couple not unlike the popular Nick and Nora Charles characters created by William Powell and Myrna Loy in "The Thin Man" movies of the thirties and forties.

It was during this era that Rock's name again came up in gossip columns. A slanderous item claimed that Rock had "married" television actor Jim Nabors in a private gay wedding ceremony. The public dismissed the story as ridiculous, but people in the industry weren't so amused. Nabors' CBS-TV variety show was promptly canceled. According to Nabors, although he and Rock were just casual friends, they could never be seen together in public again.

When *McMillan and Wife* concluded production in 1977, Rock accepted other television offers, appearing in three mini-series—*Wheels* (1978), *The Martian Chronicles* (1980), and *The Star Maker* (1981). In 1980 Rock reunited on screen with his *Giant* costar Elizabeth Taylor for the tongue-in-cheek Agatha Christie whodunit *The Mirror Crack'd*. Hudson appeared in the made-for-TV production *World War III* and a short-lived TV adventure series called *The Devlin Connection* in 1982. Throughout this period Rock maintained his solid and appealing leading-man image.

In 1984, after a two-year absence from television and movie screens, it was announced that Rock had signed to appear in ten episodes of the top-rated TV series *Dynasty*. Millions of *Dynasty* fans were thrilled by the prospect of seeing the legendary Rock as one of the stars of the glossiest, most publicized soap opera in television history. The Rock that his fans saw in the first episode was a mere ghost of the virile Rock Hudson of twenty, ten, or even two years before. He was thin and pale, and his eyes lacked the sparkle they had always projected. "Did you see Rock Hudson on *Dynasty*!" people gasped all over America, immediately speculating that Rock had fallen to the plague that was killing thousands of male homosexuals: AIDS. Statements were issued claiming that Rock had been dieting and never felt better. But the hollow cheeks and sunken eyes that *Dynasty* viewers glimpsed only increased the speculation that Rock Hudson was indeed dying of AIDS.

Ironically, it was at a press conference with his close friend and former costar Doris Day that the whole tragic scandal began to explode. It was early in July of 1985 and Rock was making his first public appearance since his last *Dynasty* episode. In the two months following the *Dynasty* filming, Rock seemed to have aged fifteen years! On Tuesday, July 23, it was front-page news that Rock had collapsed on his way to the American Hospital in Paris, where new AIDS cures were being experimentally tested.

Rock Hudson's subsequent admission of both his battle against a terminal case of AIDS and his homosexual life-style is perhaps the most magnanimous gesture the dying actor could have possibly made. Suddenly the sexually transmitted disease wasn't just an affliction striking members of society's underworld—it was an illness that could strike the most highly respected and beloved of national heroes. For four decades Rock Hudson had stood for clean-cut, all-American virtues, and as his final act, he opened the door to his long-secret private life in an effort to save the lives of others.

In the months since Rock's death, millions of dollars have been poured into discovering a cure for

AIDS. Prior to Rock's own tragic illness, AIDS was considered an affliction that was unspeakable. Even Rock's friend President Ronald Reagan would not discuss the topic of AIDS publicly, nor would he support efforts to procure sufficient governmental funds toward its cure. On October 2, 1985, however, the day that Rock died, the House of Representatives voted to provide $189.7 million toward discovering a cure for AIDS.

For more than thirty years Rock Hudson brought to life romantic screen heroes for millions of fans who idolized him. With his tragic death, Rock has become a real-life hero for thousands of individuals whose lives have been either taken or horrifyingly marred by AIDS. Rock Hudson continues to be a symbol of strength.

In his final public statement, read aloud by Burt Lancaster at a gala AIDS fund-raising benefit in Los Angeles on September 19, 1985, Rock Hudson stated: "I am not happy that I am sick. I am not happy that I have AIDS, but if that is helping others, I can, at least, know that my own misfortune has had some positive worth." Rock Hudson made his once-secret private life public in order to benefit other victims of of AIDS around the world. In a decade that has seen it all and done it all, Rock Hudson has redefined the word "star."

"Nothing's turned out like I planned.
I just feel like my saddle's turning
out from under me."
—Rock Hudson
to Elizabeth Taylor
in *Giant* (1956)

★ 1 ★
JULY 1985

ROCK HUDSON knew that he was dying of AIDS
on Monday, July 15, 1985, when he arrived in Carmel, California, for the press conference to launch
Doris Day's new television show. It had been several
months since he had completed the season's final
episode of *Dynasty*, which was destined to be his
farewell acting assignment.

In his thirty-seven years in motion pictures, Rock
Hudson portrayed as wide an assortment of characters as any actor could hope to play. He was the
moralistic soldier in *Seminole*, the wronged Indian
warrior in *Taza, Son of Cochise*, the right-wing cattle
baron in *Giant*, the carefree bachelor in *Lover Come
Back*, the psychopathic killer in *Pretty Maids All in
a Row*, the deranged genetic scientist in *Embryo*,
and the president of the United States in *World
War III*. On this particular afternoon in July, Rock
was to play his most challenging role yet . . . he was
to act as if nothing was wrong with his health. However, this performance was not only to persuade his
audience, it was also, indeed primarily, to convince
himself.

In 1978 Rock was quoted as saying, "Work keeps
me alive. I've seen so many cases of people who
retire and then die a few months later. It's manda-
tory to keep active." Never before was that statement

17

so true. It was the reason for his stint on TV's *Dynasty*, and the reason for his performance in front of the cameras on that particular day.

Rock's appearance in July 15 was skeletal compared to the Rock Hudson that movie and television viewers had known throughout his career. His weight had dropped from 195 pounds to 135 pounds, and his waist had decreased from 38 inches to 33 inches. His publicist Dale Olson, referring to Hudson's new look, claimed, "He loves it. He just threw out all his clothes and bought a new wardrobe." Rock himself had been deflecting comments on his gaunt appearance by stating that he hated the food in Israel where he had gone to film his final theatrical film, *The Ambassador,* and had been dieting ever since.

Rock's fans around the world were shocked when they saw the photos of his reunion with Doris Day plastered all over newspapers. Doris appeared as fresh and bubbly as ever, while Rock appeared to be at least twenty years her senior.

Doris had agreed to return to television to do a half-hour weekly program on CBN (Christian Broadcast Network) entitled *Doris Day's Best Friends,* and as her first guest, she chose Rock Hudson.

Not even Doris, however, was prepared for the shock that came when Rock arrived in Carmel that Monday for the television taping and the press conference. "It was a heartbreaking time for me to see him," Doris later admitted, adding that Hudson only explained to her that he had had a case of the flu, possessed no appetite, and couldn't seem to gain any of his weight back. When she got a look at him, she was concerned about his health, and she tried to dissuade him from even participating in the taping. But he told her that she had invited him to be her first guest, and he intended to be just that. With that, Doris did her best to bolster his morale, and together they faced the cameras as if nothing were wrong. Doris did not pressure him about his health again, and the next day the scheduled events went as planned.

Later, Doris took Rock's publicist Dale Olson aside and again voiced her concern. "He was not his usual bubbly self," Olson later admitted. "I didn't want him to go, and Doris said later, 'You should not have brought him.' But he's the kind of person who's very loyal. He said, 'Doris expects me. I want to go.' "

Over the next two weeks, Olson was to consistently fabricate new facts in an effort to shield Rock from the persistent rumors that he was indeed dying of AIDS. "He is in perfect health," Olson proclaimed in the July 17, 1985, issue of *U.S.A. Today,* adding that "Everybody says, 'Does he have cancer?' 'Does he have whatever?' I've asked his doctor. He's just thin."

A member of the CBN staff was later to recall, "I would never have recognized him . . . it was definitely not one of his good days."

Someone from Rock's entourage was heard to explain, "He didn't know how bad he looked. He thought he looked better than he had in a long time."

"His clothes were extremely loose fitting!" one journalist gasped, while another exclaimed, "We all sort of sat there stunned! We just felt it wasn't appropriate to ask what was wrong."

However, over the next five days, every major news outlet across America carried the photos of shockingly thin Rock and the news stories questioning his mysteriously declining health. A daily media blitz was on, and Rock's concerned fans followed each development as avidly as they followed episodes of *Dynasty.*

Olson continued to provide protective explanations: "He was very tired when those pictures were taken. . . . He hadn't slept for forty-eight hours because he had the flu. . . . As far as I know it's nothing. I saw him the day before. He seemed all right. He's going on a vacation." And finally, the most fantastic one of all: "He began losing weight. He loves the idea of being slender again."

The next day Rock boarded a jet for Paris, France. When he collapsed in his room in the Ritz Hotel and lapsed into a coma on Tuesday, July 24, his condition was front-page news: "Rock Hudson Felled by Cancer of Liver . . . Cancer Inoperable; AIDS Rumor Rejected" . . . "Rock Hudson in and out of Coma" . . . "Rock Hudson Fighting for Life."

In reality, Rock Hudson had known since June 1984 that he was dying of AIDS. He had kept his knowledge secret. In 1984 he had secretly come to Paris for AIDS treatment with experimental drugs not yet tried in the United States. Throughout his trauma he kept the fact that he was dying to himself, just as he had shielded his homosexuality from his public for all of these years.

Now what could he do? He could stick to the liver-cancer story and let his secret die with him. Surely the French doctors would not disclose his condition. He could disappear and stick to the previous announcement that he was suffering from anorexia nervosa. Or he could admit that he was gay and dying of AIDS, thus spending his last days afloat in an ocean of criticism.

True to the heroic image he had portrayed for so many years, on July 25, 1985, Rock Hudson elected to open the doors to his private life in hopes that other AIDS sufferers might benefit from his own admission. When Rock Hudson "came out of the closet," he dragged the terminal plague known as AIDS out as well.

"Through my own inadequacy, you
have missed a most wondrous part
of your life, and that's called 'growing up.' "

—Rock Hudson
to Barbara Carrera
in *Embryo* (1975)

⭐ 2 ⭐
ROY HAROLD SCHERER, JR.
(1925–1948)

WINNETKA, Illinois, is located fifteen miles north
of the heart of downtown Chicago. With a population of fourteen thousand, Winnetka is considered
an affluent suburb of the Windy City. In 1925, with
a population half that size, it was the home of Kay
Wood Scherer and her auto-mechanic husband Roy
Harold Scherer, a young couple on the lower end of
the small town's economic scale.

On Tuesday, November 17, 1925, Kay gave birth
to her first and only child, Roy Harold Scherer, Jr.
His Aunt Jessie described Roy Jr. as a "beautiful"
baby with "a sweet smile." Indeed, the child blended
the best physical attributes of his German/Swiss father and his English/Irish mother. For many years
the entire family referred to young Roy as "Junior."

When the boy was four years old, the great Depression came, and his father lost his job. Roy Sr.
soon left Kay and his son and headed west for California, for a trial separation. With no husband, and
no income, Kay divorced Scherer and began supporting herself and her young son by working as a
telephone operator.

In 1931, Kay married an ex-Marine officer Wallace Fitzgerald, and bashful Roy Jr.'s world went through one of the many changes it would undergo in his life. Fitzgerald adopted Kay's son, making him Roy Harold Fitzgerald and eliminating the "Junior" that he had grown to hate.

Life with his new stepfather was hardly an improvement. Years later Rock was simply to recall for reporters, "We didn't get along," and leave it at that.

One of his grammar-school friends, Edward Jenner, still clearly recalls growing up with Roy Fitzgerald. "We were in the same class," says Jenner. "I was the poor little rich kid, driven to public school by the chauffeur each morning. There were a bunch of hoodlum types going to the school, and they would tease and bully me. But Roy stuck up for me and told them to 'lay off.' After Roy intervened, the others accepted me. When things were tough, he was the only friend I had.

"We used to sleep over at each other's houses," continues Jenner. "When he came to my house, he was overwhelmed—we had a swimming pool, and our house was like a country club without the dues! His house had just two little bedrooms, and was tiny. At that time his mother was a telephone operator and his stepfather was a gas-station attendant."

Another boyhood friend, Mrs. Edrita Braun, recalls, "They were short of money and his home life wasn't particularly happy. His mother worked at Walgreen's for a while and then they lived above the store. It was tough on him."

Young Roy took out his frustrations by getting into childhood mischief out of the house. One of his classmates, George Crepas, remembers, "Once he put a live garter snake in a teacher's desk. She opened it and screamed like hell. She kept the whole class late that day—but nobody talked."

Liquor was another way to do something taboo. Rock was to later recall that he had his first drink "when I was nine. All of us kids did. We'd steal half-pints of whiskey from a tavern and run and drink . . . fun! I drank vanilla afterward so I wouldn't have bad breath. It was some years before I had my second—my mother found out about it!"

Kay corroborated his story, and was later to say, "Rock was pretty easy to punish. All I had to do was say he was 'stupid.' He hated the word. I didn't care what he did as long as he didn't disgrace my husband and me."

Rock's lifelong aversion to seafood could also be traced to something that happened to him in childhood. "I was nine, and my stepfather, a New Englander, took me to Maine to introduce me to a boiled fish dinner. I remember how gray all the food looked—the oysters and the other shellfish. He forced me to eat and I kept getting sick. Later he took me on a roller coaster and I was sick again. I'll never forget the day," he was later to recount.

Quarreling between Kay and her second husband became so regular that after a couple of trial separations, Roy and his mother packed up and moved in with her mother, father, brother, and sister-in-law. His aunt, Mrs. Hedwig Wood, remembered when Roy and his mother moved in. "We were a houseful," she stated. "He was always trying to make my cakes fall so I'd have to give them to him. He'd either open up the oven or stomp around the kitchen to ruin the baking. And he'd eat the whole cake by himself. His favorite was spice."

Hudson's Aunt Jessie also recalled, "When he was eight or nine he used to do the marketing. He'd go to the grocery store with a list his mother had prepared, and if he happened to see a bargain he'd buy it whether it was on the list or not. He'd not only bring the food home, but if the potatoes needed paring or there were onions to be peeled or a roast to be put in the oven, he'd have them all done by the time his mother returned."

When he was ten years old, Roy got his first job, delivering the *Chicago Daily News*. He was remembered by one of his customers as "a cute little fellow, forever smiling. He had dreamy eyes and never seemed to be in a hurry."

Looking back on his childhood in Winnetka, Rock later said, "We weren't exactly poor. Even if we had been, we wouldn't have starved—too many relatives in town!

"There were ten of us squeezed into this small, five-room, white stucco house on Center Street in Winnetka," he explained. "Times were very hard for us. Times were hard for most everyone during the Depression. I started doing odd jobs by the time I was twelve, so I could help out. I was a caddy, a soda jerker, a window washer, a short-order cook. Once I worked for a shade and awning firm. In the winter they removed the awnings from the rich houses and stored them away. I was in charge of labeling and storing the awnings. I forgot to label them. When spring rolled around, they had difficulties trying to figure out which awnings belonged to which houses.

"One thing that made it hard for me living in Winnetka was that it was a suburb of well-to-do families. Many of the boys and girls I knew at school lived in large homes with all the luxuries. I had no spending money as a rule. I was a typical high-school adolescent. I was average in school. My grade average was under a B-plus. I sang in the school glee club and in the choir of the First Congregational Church. I sang soprano because my voice refused to change. When I had time and a little change in my pockets, I hung around with a nice gang of boys and girls, drinking sodas or dancing in nearby Evanston. I admired swing and boogie-woogie piano," said Rock.

When he was growing up, his most important relationship was with his mother. "She raised me," he later explained. "So, she was mother, big sister, big brother to me, and best friend. I to her: the same. I had to be big brother or little brother, son, confidant, all that. She rarely had to spank me as a little kid. She always said, 'Never make a fool of yourself, and more importantly, never embarrass me.' Regardless of who she was married to, we always had a great affection for one another."

One of young Roy's practical jokes was played on his mother, when he was supposed to be painting the walls of the bathroom of their home. According to childhood friend Mrs. Nancy Burnet, "His mother asked him to paint the bathroom wall, but he apparently got carried away. He ended up painting everything—fixtures, bathtub, sink—a purplish blue. His mother was, to say the least, rather cross."

When he was twelve years old, something happened to Rock that would change his life. While watching a 1937 Dorothy Lamour movie Roy decided what he was going to do with his life . . . he wsa going to become a movie star! "It was a late-thirties movie called *The Hurricane*," he was to recall over and over again. "I saw that picture twenty-five times just to watch Jon Hall dive into the ocean from the mast of a schooner. I watched him, and I said, 'That's what I'm gonna be—a movie star who does exciting things like that.'

"I tried out for school plays, but couldn't seem to remember lines, and I looked like a pencil—six feet, four inches tall, and only 150 pounds. At the time I put that dive away in my head and remembered it, but I didn't go very far in high-school drama. I went to high school in Evanston, Illinois, and I tried to be in the school's plays, but . . . I was so terrible they threw me out, but I still did the Christmas pageants. I was one of the Three Wise Men beside a cardboard camel singing 'We Three Kings of Orient Are,' only I pronounced it 'Orien Tar!' I never told anybody, 'I want to be an actor when I grow up.'" But for several years to come, young Roy would carry with him this secret desire. He didn't even let his mother in on his private career ambition, rationalizing that, "I suppose if I told her that I was thinking about being an actor, she'd say, 'Oh, what do you want to do that for!'"

New Trier High School is known for being the alma mater for several show-business personalities, including Ann-Margret and Ralph Bellamy. Rock recalled, "I was in the same class at New Trier as Hugh O'Brien, and just a year behind Charlton Heston. But neither one of them remembers me from high school, and I don't blame them a bit. There was nothing to remember. The worst of it was I was scared. I was scared of people. I was scared of performing in front of people. I didn't have any confidence in myself. I was scared I would not be good enough—that I did not understand the character or the mood or the scene."

His cousin Marjory Kuipers later stated, "When he was sixteen, he had a real crush on Lana Turner. But it was a surprise to me when HE became a star. He couldn't act—he had no talent, he couldn't do anything!"

After Roy and his mother moved out of their relatives' house, all of Roy's friends were welcome at their new home for afterschool get-togethers. One of his high-school classmates, Doreen Fisher, remembered that Roy was great at the latest craze: dancing the Jitterbug. "Roy was good at it," she said. "He was always buying Jitterbug records and we'd go over to his house and dance. His mother was really friendly and didn't mind having the crowd troop in on her." Roy's favorite record at that time was the Andrews Sisters' "Rum Boogie," which was played over and over again on the hand-wound Victrola he owned.

Rock later recalled the great rapport he had with his mother. "I remember when I was seventeen years old and wanted to take the car on Saturday nights, I'd have to get her mad first. Then I'd throw both arms around her and hold her so she couldn't move and say, 'Now what are you going to do?' She'd break up laughing and give me the keys to the car."

Roy graduated from high school in 1943 and landed a job as a substitute carrier for the post office. For seven months, for $1.25 an hour, he worked on his route from six-thirty in the morning until four in the afternoon. In January 1944, Roy's carrier's outfit was turned in for a United States Navy uniform, when he was drafted into service. After his training he was sent to the South Pacific.

One of his most dramatic stories about the war was invented for the sake of his Hollywood press agent years later. Rock is quoted as stating, "I worked on Corsairs and TBFs" referring to the planes he was responsible for. "When the war was over, they transferred me to bombers. One morning I was checking a four-engine job. Nobody told me it was dangerous to rev up both motors on the same side at once. That plane jumped the chocks blocking her front wheels. Before I brought the big bomber to a dead stop, her propellers sliced a Piper Cub into kindling wood. The next day I was transferred to laundry detail." Eleven years later, a full-fledged movie star, he no longer had to make up stories for press releases, and admitted, "I made up that one, along with a lot of other stories. Publicity people wanted exciting anecdotes and I didn't have any."

The only true part was the information about the laundry detail. "The war was over and I still had four months to go," he admitted. "The officers gave you liquor for taking care of all their uniforms, and the energetic guy could pick up forty to fifty dollars a week just by going through the pockets of their dirty uniforms."

Roy was discharged in San Francisco in May 1946, and he took what money he had, bought a car, and headed home. "After my discharge I returned to Winnetka. I wanted a vacation. For nearly a year I just drifted around, drawing down my twenty dollars a week from the government. When the checks stopped coming, I took a civil-service examination for a post office job. I passed and soon started carrying the mail. I stood about three months of it and then my feet and back started begging for mercy. I talked it over with my mother. My father and I had been writing letters back and forth. He now lived in Long Beach, a few miles from Los Angeles, where he owned an electrical-appliance store. My father said I could stay with him . . . until I decided what I wanted to do.

"Even after I'd been in the navy, I still had the acting bug. After an inner struggle whether to go to New York and try for the stage or come to Los Angeles and take a stab at motion pictures, I made up my mind to come out here [L.A.] and study drama at USC."

The plan went a bit awry, however. First of all, the University of Southern California was being flooded with applications from discharged GIs, and it raised its entrance standards to a "B-plus." Roy Fitzgerald's grade-point average wasn't up to the university's standards. The second blow to his aspirations came when he brought up the subject of acting to his father. "You know any . . . uh . . . movie actors?" Roy Jr.

asked, figuring that everyone within a fifty-mile radius of Hollywood had to know at least one of the stars. Roy Sr. made a funny face, "Junior," would recall, "like I had hit him in the stomach. 'Don't mention actors to me,' he said. 'They're unreliable and unstable!' "

Rock would later tell how he gave his father's business a try. "For a while I worked for him part-time, trying to sell tank-type vacuum cleaners house to house, but if anybody said 'no,' I took the 'no' as a final answer. I carried the vacuum and the extra set of attachments in my hands. I hung a long flexible tube around my neck. I'd go to a door, and when the housewife opened it, I'd say, 'You don't want to buy a vacuum cleaner, do you?' Naturally she'd say 'no,' and I'd say, 'Okay,' and walk on to the next house. One woman volunteered to let me give her a demonstration. I vacuumed her whole house. I even vacuumed her car, but when I was done, all she said was, 'Thank you. I'm not buying anything.' So I told my dad, 'I'm afraid I have to have another job. I've got to make at least a little money.' He called somebody he knew and landed me a job driving a truck delivering dried food. I held that job for six months."

Roy was certain that he wanted to stay in California. "When I got a load of the sunshine and the palm trees and the smog, I knew this was where I wanted to live." But driving a truck wasn't getting him any closer to his goal of breaking into the movies.

Thinking that a new outfit would be the right thing to catch people's attention, Roy walked into a men's store and a certain gabardine suit grabbed his attention. "First suit I ever bought with a coat and trousers that matched," he said. "Cost fifty-five dollars. I'm so tall I had to have terrific alterations made in it. The pants were so big that when I had them taken in, there was almost no distance between the hip pockets, and they couldn't cut it down enough so I could wear it with a belt. I had to use suspenders. It was a double-breasted suit, and I didn't dare unbutton it—the pants would have ballooned out as if inflated. After I got the suit, I braced myself one night and told my new friends, 'I want to be an actor.' Nobody laughed. They said, 'Why not?' A couple of them even made suggestions.

"I roomed with three other truck drivers in a family hotel in Westlake Park. One of the truck drivers had a friend who had a friend who knew a man named Henry Willson, who was in charge of talent for David O. Selznick. At the time Selznick had his own studio. I asked this friend of my friend's friend how somebody could get into the movies. When he saw I was on the level, he said to get some photographs made and then he would arrange an appointment with Willson. I went to a woman photographer in Hollywood. She took five different poses of me. The pictures cost twenty-five dollars and I had to work three days on the truck to pay for them. I dropped the pictures off at Willson's office. Next day I went to see him."

The meeting that day in the spring of 1948 was to put Roy Fitzgerald onto the road he sought. It was quite beyond him at the time why Willson even gave him an interview. "The Lord only knows why," he later recalled. "I was still skinny, I still had a squeaky little voice, and went slouching around trying to look shorter than I was. I was also painfully shy and knew absolutely nothing about acting. I tell you, I didn't so much walk into Henry Willson's office as shamble in sideways, with my knees knocking."

When Willson asked Fitzgerald to sit down, Roy did so, and when he attempted to say "Thanks," he was so nervous that "No sounds came out of my mouth!" he remembered. "He shuffled my photographs around like they were a poker hand. Then he glanced at me and said, 'You're not bad looking.' I said 'Thanks.' 'Can you act?' he asked. 'No,' I said, and stood up. I figured the interview was over."

Willson asked, "What did you say, feller?"

Fitzgerald replied, "I said, 'no,' I can't act."

"Good!" exclaimed Willson. "Then I think I can do something for you."

Willson explained to young Fitzgerald that the Selznick Studios were about to be dissolved and that he would soon be out of a job. However, he was about to go into business for himself, starting his own agency. Would Roy like to become his first client? Naturally Roy jumped at the opportunity.

Henry Willson began introducing Roy to all of his studio contacts, in hopes that he would find his new discovery film work. Rock was later to remember, "Among the various places he took me was Twentieth Century–Fox, where I made a screen test. It was so bad that it was shown to beginner classes as an example of how not to act! And I met Louis B. Mayer, the head man of Metro—upside down. He was in a barber's chair having his face steamed. Some idiot in Metro's casting office told me, 'You've got to meet Mr. Mayer.' So, off we went, over to the barbershop, and there he was. He said, 'How do you do?' That was all! The barber slapped the towel back on his face. After that, Willson took me to Warner Brothers to be interviewed, and I met the director Raoul Walsh."

Walsh was about to start a picture entitled "Fighter Squadron," and Roy was perfect for a small speaking part in it. Walsh not only wanted Roy in the film, he wanted to sign the young man to a personal-development contract. The twenty-two-year-old aspiring actor was just what he was looking for . . . except for that name: Roy Fitzgerald. It just didn't have the right pizzazz.

It was Willson who came up with the new moniker for his young discovery . . . he would call him "Rock Hudson"! According to Willson, "When I first saw him, I was awfully impressed with his size. I thought of the biggest thing around, and the Rock of Gibraltar is what came to mind. The 'Hudson' part just came along, I guess from the river. 'Rock Hudson' just seemed to fit him."

The ploy was so successful that Willson later changed Arthur Gelien into Tab Hunter, Francis McGowan into Rory Calhoun, Robert Moseley into Guy Madison, Merle Johnson, Jr., into Troy Donahue, and Jimmy Ercolani into James Dean.

However, Willson's main claim to fame is for taking an ambitious young truck driver from the Midwest and turning him into a movie star that the world would come to know as Rock Hudson.

> "Gentlemen, everything I told you is the truth."
>
> —Rock Hudson
> in *Seminole* (1953)

★ 3 ★
ENTER ROCK HUDSON
1948–1954

HENRY WILLSON is credited with shaping ambitious Roy Fitzgerald into a screen commodity. Even though he had been rechristened Rock Hudson, the young man didn't know the first thing about being a professional movie actor. Rock was later to discuss Willson's influence by explaining, "He said I should take acting lessons, and that they'd cost twenty-five dollars an hour. I told him I couldn't afford it, but he replied, 'I'll pay—and don't thank me.'"

One prominent show-business agent who knew him personally recalls, "Rock Hudson was a very simple-minded man fascinated with being an actor." Indeed, there was quite a fear at first that although Rock was extremely handsome, he wasn't too bright. When Willson took Hudson to meet powerful film producer Walter Wanger, Rock was instructed to add a couple of years to his young age of twenty-two but didn't know how many fictitious birthdays he should add. When Wanger asked Rock how old he was, Hudson turned to Willson and innocently inquired, "How old am I?"

Wanger frostily dismissed Hudson, and advised Willson, "Bring him back when he knows something ... when he has confidence."

It was clear that what Rock Hudson needed the

most was experience, on-the-job training, and that is exactly what he was to receive in *Fighter Squadron* (1948).

Rock's first film starred Edmond O'Brien as a dedicated combat flier in World War II in Great Britain. The second lead was Robert Stack. Stack later spoke of the "green" young actor who was to become a lifelong friend: "I met Rock on the movie *Fighter Squadron*. It was his first movie. He was a protégé of Raoul Walsh. He was a rank beginner. I think Raoul had taken him out of a truck and put him in, 'cause God knows he was handsome enough. Later on I got to know him very well."

Rock had four lines of dialogue in the war film's several group scenes. In a gambling scene in the barracks, Rock is seen slapping his wallet down on the gambling table and proclaiming, "All that says he doesn't." When another soldier puts his leather jacket on the table, Rock asks, "What's that for?" The other soldier replies, "Since you're betting leather!" In another scene Rock, referring to the squadron's mascot black cat, asks Tom D'Andrea, "Are you sure it's the right one?"

However, by far, Rock's most famous line in the movie is one that he completely screwed up. In response to a written running tally of the squadron's victories, Rock's line was to be: "Pretty soon you're going to have to get a bigger blackboard." On his first take, Rock blurted out, "Pretty soon you're going to have to get a bligger backboard." It was an easy enough mistake to make, so Walsh simply ordered, "Take two." Nervous and embarrassed by his error, Rock blew the line again ... and again ... and again. After a reported thirty-eight takes, Rock was still mumbling "bligger backboard." Finally Walsh ordered a rewrite of Rock's line and it appears in the final print of the film as "Pretty soon you're going to have to write smaller numbers"—and is delivered off-camera.

Recalled Rock: "I worked for seven or eight weeks at a hundred and twenty dollars a week. I thought it was big. I'd been making sixty!"

He was never to forget that damned "blackboard" line. Looking back on *Fighter Squadron*, he would later moan, "I was a disaster. And for a year after that I didn't appear in a picture. But I kept studying.

"That's how I got started," said Rock. "After that, Walsh put me under personal contract. For a solid year I took dramatic and diction lessons and tried to shuck my midwestern accent."

After he had completed his work on his first film as a glorified extra, Raoul Walsh gave him some much-needed advice. "Always be natural," said the seasoned director. "Don't try to act. Don't exaggerate. Remember, up on that screen you're magnified forty times or more. Underplay, and it always looks great." In addition, Walsh suggested, "Wear your hair long. You never know when you'll be cast in a western!"

Henry Willson invested three thousand dollars of his own money into his new discovery, and he sent Rock to several acting classes. According to Hudson, "We used to do whole scenes from plays and scripts, and especially something called *Hedda Gabler*—you know, like Hedda Hopper—by a guy named Ibsen. It was the dullest stuff you ever heard!"

In the meantime, his mother, Kay Fitzgerald, had moved west to California and landed a job in Pasadena as a telephone operator. Rock managed to keep his new identity as an actor a secret from her—until *Fighter Squadron* was released.

The week the film premiered, Rock simply called his mother and asked her if she wanted to go to the movies with him. Naturally, she accepted, never suspecting her son was in the film. Rock remembered being nervous, and laughingly recounted, "The picture opened at Warner's Hollywood and I was sitting there and watching the screen, and I hadn't seen the film either, so of course I was looking too."

According to Rock, his mother kept looking at the actor on the screen and back at her son in the seat next to her. She finally turned to him and asked, "That you?"

"Yeah, that's me," he replied, not knowing what her opinion of his new occupation was to be.

She simply looked back at him and said, "I see."

"She had no idea," said Hudson of his little surprise, "she thought I was still driving a truck!"

As a result of *Fighter Squadron*, Warner Brothers offered Rock a short-term contract, paying $210 a week, but Willson made the decision for his client to turn it down, afraid it would only lead to meaningless bit parts.

Rock continued his acting classes and vocal training. Since he wasn't signed to Warners but was on Raoul Walsh's payroll, Walsh decided to get his money's worth out of Hudson, and he had Rock paint his house gloss white!

When a case of laryngitis caused Rock's voice to be temporarily lower, he suddenly discovered that he could effect a more commanding vocal register with very little effort. Soon he chucked the nasal midwestern twang he had grown up with. "I stopped my lessons right there," he remembered.

"In 1949, Raoul Walsh sold my contract to Universal . . . and that's where the really good things started to happen," Rock was later to explain. The decision to go with Universal-International (U-I) was a simple matter of business—although two other studios expressed interest in Hudson, only Universal-International was willing to reimburse Willson and Walsh the $9500 they had spent on Rock's training. Rock was in good company, earning $125 a week along with the studio's other aspiring contract players, such as Jeff Chandler, Tony Curtis, Piper Laurie, Julia Adams, Richard Long, and Rod McKuen.

One of the great things about the "studio system" of the twenties, thirties, forties, and fifties was the way the studios handled new talent. When the studios signed young actors, they also groomed, trained, and educated them to become box-office successes. Rock Hudson was truly one of the last great successes of this now-extinct system of nurturing new talent.

Looking back in 1985 to those days on the Universal-International lot, Rock was to point out, "I had it lucky. Any kinds of lessons you chose were free—drama, diction, voice, horseback riding, ballet, sword fighting, gymnastics. Go out and pay for that now! Where and how do kids learn and still make a living today?

"When I signed with Universal, I studied with Sophie Rosenstein. She was drama, acting, and diction coach combined. She never told me how to read a line. She taught me, 'If you think properly, your line will come out believably,' " said Rock.

In addition to refining him and instilling confidence about the words that came out of his mouth, the studio also improved the look of his mouth. At the expense of the studio, Rock had seven of his front teeth capped. After that, he possessed the smile that girls were soon to swoon for.

Rock's first Universal film was *Undertow* (1949). The film starred Scott Brady as a gambler who is wrongly accused of murder and who, with the help of a schoolmarm played by Peggy Dow, attempts to prove his innocence. Rock's role was simply entitled "Detective."

In his third film, *I Was a Shoplifter* (1950), Rock again played a detective to Scott Brady's lead. Both Brady and Hudson are out to break up a ring of shoplifters in the flick. This was also one of Tony Curtis's first films; the young actor appeared under the name Anthony Curtis. Rock's role was simply "Store Detective."

Next came *One Way Street* (1950). James Mason starred as a dishonest doctor. Dan Duryea played Mason's gangster rival, and Rock played a truck driver. Talk about ending up right back where he started!

His next film was his first "Grade A" movie— *Winchester '73* (1950) with Jimmy Stewart and Shelley Winters. The film is about a certain Winchester '73 rifle and the series of people who own it, much like the 1965 film *Yellow Rolls Royce*. The rifle starts as Jimmy Stewart's and soon becomes the possession of an Indian chief named Young Bull. You guessed it—Rock Hudson plays Young Bull!

"I even had a putty nose in an effort to make me look like an Indian," Rock later confided. In the film he appears naked to the waist, covered with bronzer, and wears a long wig braided with pigtails and feathers. It isn't long before Young Bull is shot, and the 1873 rifle again changes hands. Tony Curtis is featured in this film, too, which marked a decided upgrade in the films on Rock's growing résumé.

Hudson's sixth film, *Peggy* (1950), also represented growth in his new career. Although the flick is the lightweight tale of a young girl named Peggy (Diana Lynn) who decides to enter the competition for the crown of Queen of the Tournament of Roses, it made Rock into a fledgling "teen idol." Portraying the Ohio State quarterback Johnny Higgins, Rock kissed Diana Lynn on the screen, and young girls sighed. Universal suddenly received fan letters, begging for much more of that handsome Rock Hudson.

Prompted by sudden interest in this newcomer, the publicity department began to give a bit of a build-up to Rock. *Peggy* brought him to the attention of the young moviegoing public, which was to be the mainstay of his early career. "It was right then that we started to get requests about Rock," said Betty Mitchell of the U-I publicity department.

Rock's personal biography was rather drab, so the story about Rock accidentally wrecking the navy plane was made up. Playing on the fact that he had once been a post office carrier, the story of his coming to the attention of Henry Willson was altered to the point where a new version found Rock as the mailman who delivered his own résumé and was discovered while presenting the package containing his photos to Willson.

Rock was later to confess, "So many of these stories are made up. The publicity departments will figure out a story and make people believe them. Like Lana Turner supposedly discovered in a drugstore. I heard the other day, 'She believes now that she WAS discovered in a drugstore!' " Another story fabricated at this time claimed that Rock used to rush through his truck route, put on his new gabardine suit, and stand outside the studio gates awaiting "discovery" by a producer. He was later to dismiss the tale by admitting that the press releases were "lies, all lies. But if I stood across from the gates of any studios, it was strictly a matter of star worship—trying to see someone famous in person."

The early publicity photos of Rock Hudson of course featured handsome headshots of the young actor. But whenever they could get Rock's shirt off, photographers would do so. In the early 1950s there were countless photos of shirtless Rock eating breakfast, washing his car, choosing a record out of his vast platter collection, or frying an egg—barefoot and in a pair of shorts. It wasn't long before the movie fan magazines picked up on Rock, and he was dubbed "the beefcake king" and "baron of the beefcake."

One of his first "fan mag" appearances came in the October 1950 issue of *Modern Screen,* in an article called "Stag Night at the Steamroom." Along with Scott Brady, John Bromfield, Hugh O'Brien, and Tony Curtis, Rock was seen in the photos wearing nothing but a small towel. When someone in the article complained about the heat in the steam room at the Finlandia Spa, Rock quipped, "You don't have the right attitude. Take a look at this boy!"

Rock was later to look back at this era and comment, "They used to have me strip to the waist for photographs. Then they'd have me dial the telephone with my muscles bulging. Good God!"

The press also liked to dwell on Rock's personal life. The first girl that he was publicly, and supposedly privately, involved in was the singer/dancer Vera-Ellen, who is best remembered as Rosemary Clooney's sister in *White Christmas* (1954). One night in 1949, Rock was having a drink with Henry Willson at the popular Hollywood nightclub Ciro's when he spotted Vera-Ellen on the dance floor with a date. Willson convinced Rock to cut in on the dance and introduce himself. And so he did! Rock and Vera-Ellen became friends and had several public dates. The Press Photographer's Costume Ball was coming up (October 1949), and Rock and Vera-Ellen came up with the idea of dressing as "Mr. and Mrs. Oscar"—the Academy Award statuettes. With plastic heads, bathing suits, swords from the prop department, and a covering of gold paint, they were the hit of the party and won First Prize for the best costumes of the evening. Rock reportedly proposed marriage but was flatly turned down. In the early 1950s, a "heartbroken" Rock proclaimed to the press, "I am terribly fond of her still, but we do not plan a marriage. Our careers are more important than love, children, and a happy marriage."

Rock's seventh film was *The Desert Hawk* (1950), the first of four films that he would appear in with Yvonne De Carlo. However, in this movie, she was the star, and Rock received tenth billing. In this Arabian tale, he portrayed Captain Ras, who unsuccessfully protects Princess Shaharazade (De Carlo), from leading man Omar (Richard Greene). Also in the cast was Jackie Gleason as Aladdin—years before he broke into successful TV comedy in *The Honeymooners*.

Next came *Shakedown* (1950), which starred Howard Duff and Peggy Dow in the tale of an unscrupulous photographer who is willing to do anything to get ahead. Rock is only seen in a bit part.

In the autumn of 1950 Rock left Hollywood for his first extensive location work, on the western *Tomahawk* (1951). While the cast was working on the film near Rapid City, South Dakota, Universal's publicity department found out that a new movie theater was about to open and figured that this would be an excellent opportunity for media coverage. The movie's stars, Van Heflin, Yvonne De Carlo, Preston Foster, and Jack Oakie all consented to help inaugurate the new theater, but when he was invited to be the fifth star on the bill at the gala, Rock was mortified at the prospect of appearing live in front of an audience.

"Why should I go on stage?" Hudson argued. "They don't know me, and I have nothing to say." After much discussion, the publicist finally convinced him to make the brief stage appearance. Rock later recalled, "He was giving me credit for a little more sense than I had. I was a dumb kid. Dumb!"

The night of the event, Heflin, De Carlo, Foster, and Oakie all came out on stage, greeted the audience, said a few words, and returned to the wings. Finally, it was Rock's turn to face the audience. According to Rock, "I walked out on stage, terrified. I finally reached the center and stood in front of the microphones. The houselights were on and I could see every individual face in the audience. I managed to get out, 'Good evening, ladies and gentlemen . . .' and then I froze." Totally stunned by the faces staring back at him, he went totally blank, and after a long silence, Jack Oakie went back out on stage and led zombielike Hudson to the safety of the wings! Rock remembered, "I walked like a robot, still in trauma!"

Tomahawk, which was released in early 1951, dealt with the conflicts between Indians and the settlers in the 1860s. In this standard cowboy and Indian flick, Rock portrays a soldier named Burt Hanna, who falls in love with an Indian maiden named Monahseetah (Susan Cabot).

Rock's tenth film was *Air Cadet* (1951), and he had the role of "Upper Classman" to Stephen McNally's portrayal of the instructor. It was followed by *The Fat Man* (1951), which was a "film noir" screen adaptation of a 1945 radio series created by Dashiell Hammett. J. Scott Smart played the title role and Rock was one of the gangsters who must deal with $500,000 in stolen loot. However, Hudson's character learns too late that crime does not pay.

Next came *Iron Man* (1951) in which Rock portrays Speed O'Keefe, the boxing best friend of boxer Coke Mason (Jeff Chandler). Rock landed this role because he had been working out with the Universal-International studio trainer Frankie Van, who was helping Hudson to broaden his shoulders and develop his forearms. According to Van, "Rock needed a lot of deltoid development, across the shoulders, and bigger forearms. But his legs and his rear were perfect. When he came he couldn't recognize a pair of boxing gloves. In six weeks I had him down to 191 pounds from 202, and he was more Gene Tunney than Gene Tunney!"

On the day that eight studio executives were testing a group of contract players for the boxing role of Speed O'Keefe, Rock came in with Van issuing instructions. Pitting Rock against a semipro in the ring, Van coached Hudson. "Look: left, right, left-right—then a left hook, and then he goes down." Overanxious, Rock knocked his surprised opponent to the floor on his second punch and was promptly awarded the part in *Iron Man*. Hudson later bragged, "After that, I figured I had the right to be sure of myself!"

Bright Victory (1951) was the fifth picture that Rock appeared in that year. "I was only in the first nine pages of the script," he admitted. The film was again a "Grade A" production in which Rock played a minor character. It was a touching story starring Arthur Kennedy as a World War II veteran who loses his eyesight in battle. Kennedy received an Academy Award nomination for his acting and won the title of "Best Actor of 1951" from the New York Film Critics. Much of the filming took place at Veteran's Hospital in Valley Forge, Pennsylvania. Although his part was small, it was a prestigious film for Rock to appear in.

It was while working on *Bright Victory* that Rock first became acquainted with a pretty young blond girl named Betty Abbott. She worked as a script girl at Universal and was the niece of Bud Abbott of the comedy team Abbott and Costello. After that Rock and Betty attended several public functions together.

Since the Hollywood gossip columnists were constantly bugging him about who he was dating, Rock issued a statement about Betty to get them off his back. "She's a striking-looking girl with warmth and understanding and a rare gift for gaiety." That hardly sounds like undying passion.

Henry Willson saw that his client was moving along nicely with his film career; if he played his cards right, Rock Hudson would soon become a household name. Willson took him out to plays like *Annie Get Your Gun,* and to parties to meet and mingle with such contemporaries as Van Johnson.

On one occasion Gary Cooper's wife Rocky telephoned Willson to see if Rock would be available to escort her to a social event. Soon Rock was being seen and photographed at the right places with the right people. The studio executives began to take notice of the attention their young "charge" was receiving and commanded him to purchase a tuxedo, a dark blue serge suit, a gray plaid suit, and a gray-and-blue gabardine suit—all at their expense. "It must have cost them a fortune!" exclaimed Rock. "I went to the best tailor in town—I think!"

Rock was steadily gaining confidence in his career, and he felt he was capable of taking a greater responsibility in shaping it. When he learned that Universal was planning to do a film adaptation of the book *Fidler's Green,* he felt that he would be perfect in one of the roles. He had read the book, and one day he mustered up the courage to pay a visit to the office of studio head Rufus LeMaire. According to Rock, "I walked into the office, full of authority, and said, 'I'd like to play the part of the guy who's in love with the murderer's moll.' LeMaire asked, 'Why?' and I said, 'Oh, I don't know,' and turned around and walked out!" The film adaptation was entitled *The Raging Tide,* and was made without Rock Hudson.

Although he was obviously not a big enough "name" to pick and choose his own roles, Rock was winning the confidence of his coworkers. At the time, according to Sophie Rosenstein, the U-I drama coach, "His big asset was simply stamina. His biggest failing was shyness. It was torture for him to act before an audience, but he kept on doing it. He talked too fast; he didn't stand up straight; he put his head down like a bull and looked out from under his eyebrows. But he never had any vanity and was always willing to learn. Sincerity was the hardest thing he had to learn—to mean the lines he was saying."

Indeed, stamina was one of Rock's decidedly strong points in those days. During one stretch in 1951, he worked in front of the movie cameras every single day for five consecutive months without a break. He was seen in five films in 1951, and in 1952, he was in six separate motion pictures. His only comment was, "I asked for work when I signed up—and I got it. And it's paying off, so why should I complain?"

Rock's fourteenth film was *Here Come the Nelsons* (1952), which was a big-screen release based on the radio and television adventures of Ozzie and Harriet Nelson and their two sons, David and Ricky. Of all the offbeat things for Rock to portray, in this film he played Charles Jones—a brassiere salesman!

His next part was in *Bend of the River* (1952), as a gambler named Trey Wilson. The film starred Jimmy Stewart as the hero and Arthur Kennedy as the villain. When the movie was released, Rock got one of his first review mentions, in *The New York Times,* which found him to be "ornamental as a gentleman gambler." Not exactly a rave, but a mention nonetheless.

In January 1952, *Bend of the River* premiered in Portland, Oregon, where much of the principal photography was shot. The night of the gala premiere, the stars arrived at the theater in a long procession through the streets of Portland. James Stewart, Arthur Kennedy, Julia Adams, and Rock Hudson all rode in separate convertibles with their names painted on the sides of the cars. Rock was in shock when members of the crowd of thousands of star-struck moviegoers began chanting, "We want Rock! We want Rock Hudson!" He was pleasurably awed and later explained, "I'm willing to bet they [Universal] gave two hundred kids a dollar each to start the chant. Later I accused them of it, but they denied it was a stunt."

In his next film, *Scarlet Angel* (1953), Rock attained a new high point in his career as THE leading man in a picture. Although Yvonne De Carlo was the undisputed star of the film, Hudson reached a new status with his second billing. The movie was a remake of the studio's hit *Flame of New Orleans* (1941), which had starred Marlene Dietrich and Bruce Cabot. Yvonne plays an aggressive vixen from the wrong side of the tracks who has clawed her way up the social ladder but falls for a rough-around-the-edges ship's captain played by Rock.

Has Anybody Seen My Gal? (1952) found Rock in the roaring twenties as a soda jerk to Piper Laurie's society girl who falls in love with him. Rock gets to dance a frenetic Charleston in this film, and if you look quick, you can catch James Dean in a bit part. Four years later, both Hudson and Dean were to be nominated for Academy Awards in *Giant*.

Has Anybody Seen My Gal? was also an important step in Rock's career, as it was the first of his films to be directed by Douglas Sirk, who was to direct him in eight more (including *Magnificent Obsession, All That Heaven Allows,* and *Written on the Wind*). Sirk began in German cinema productions, and according to Rock, "He didn't have total command of the English language. When he was directing a crowd scene for *Has Anybody Seen My Gal?* he would say,

'All right, people. Remember, this is a comedy!' Now, what does that mean? Incidentally, James Dean was in that film, too, in a very small role, with slicked-back wavy hair, very neatly combed. He [Sirk] was a good director. And I'd say that *Written on the Wind* and *Tarnished Angels* were important movies."

Horizons West (1952) found Robert Ryan and Rock Hudson as brothers who return from the Civil War to their Texas rancher family. Rock plays Neal Hammond, the good brother who becomes a lawman. Ryan plays Dan Hammond, the outlaw who wants more than an honest living can offer him, so he turns to crime.

It was on *Horizons West* that Rock first worked with director Budd Boetticher. According to Boetticher at the time, "Rock is just a big kick-the-dirt boy, a bashful lover. He's best when he grins. The hardest scenes he does are the serious ones. He blows a lot of lines, but he always says he's sorry, and means it."

The Lawless Breed (1952) was Rock's nineteenth film and was the first in which he received top billing. The film, which reunited him with his first director, Raoul Walsh, was a successfully entertaining adaptation of the autobiography of 1870s Texas outlaw John Wesley Hardin. Rock plays the real-life gunman who returns home from a sixteen-year prison sentence to find that his young son idolizes his father's criminal past and is on the road to ruin. In the end, Rock's character convinces his mixed-up son that crime doesn't pay. The working title of this film was *The Texas Man,* but the title was changed to *The Lawless Breed* before its release.

For Rock Hudson, 1952 was a very important year. In his last six films, he had gone from a featured actor to a leading man. After work on his twentieth film, *Seminole* (1953), his U-I contract came up for renewal. He signed a new contract which began him at a salary of a thousand dollars a week, with salary escalation clauses that would end with him earning nearly four thousand a week. The contract also stipulated that he would be immediately loaned out to his old boss Raoul Walsh for an RKO film entitled *Sea Devils* (1953) and a Columbia film called *Gun Fury* (1953). All it would take was the right vehicle, and screen stardom was sure to be his.

Rock's monthly fan mail had reached a new high in volume. When *Peggy* was released in March 1950, he received fourteen fan letters. In July 1952 he was up to a grand total of 1800 a month. By the end of the year, his monthly total of fan mail had reached nearly four thousand.

Considering the diversity of the roles that Rock had portrayed in his first five years in Hollywood, he was one of the most versatile young actors at the Universal-International studio. Rock's makeup man Burris Grimwood proclaimed at that time, "Of course we have to stipple in hair for him—mustache, beard, sideburns—since he can't grow it himself. We darken his prominent Adam's apple a bit, so it won't show so much. We might have to tape back his ears later. He has his own windblown hairdo; we just let it go."

Looking back at the body of his film work, Rock commented with a sense of humor, "All my parts seem to be in the Southwest. I wish I could get something in the Northeast." Examining his own screen image, circa 1952, he stated, "I don't like myself on the screen; I get embarrassed in the projection room. I can't make love very well; I just go in and mash the makeup. Riding is okay, but horses still don't take to me—one threw me counterclockwise the other day." Rumors were already beginning to circulate around Hollywood in 1952 that twenty-seven-year-old Hudson was a "confirmed bachelor." Nosy gossip columnist Louella Parsons was already prying. According to Louella, she asked him, "Haven't you ever been in love or thought of getting married?" To which Rock answered, "Don't you remember that Vera-Ellen and I were once engaged and very much in love?" Louella reported to her millions of readers, "Rock likes it this way, too—not being married, I mean. He told me he won't marry any girl until he is better situated financially nor while his career is still in the growing stage."

To commemorate his newfound success, Rock went to Detroit to buy himself a brand-new yellow Lincoln Continental convertible, fresh off the assembly line. He drove from Detroit to Chicago to join his mother, who was visiting old friends and relatives, then the two of them returned to California in Rock's new car.

When the *Motion Picture Herald* announced their 1952 "Stars of Tomorrow," Rock was on the list along with Marilyn Monroe, Audie Murphy, and Marge and Gower Champion. By the end of the year Universal Studios estimated that they had already invested $5 million in Rock Hudson, in salaries, film footage, and publicity expenses. One could say that at that point in time, Rock Hudson was U-I's "Five Million Dollar Man."

On December 17, 1952, much to his own surprise, Rock Hudson was the guest of honor on the television show *This Is Your Life*. Taped before a "live" studio audience in the El Capitan Theater in Hollywood, Rock was in shock when the host/announcer Ralph Edwards turned the cameras onto the audience and asked, "Where is Mr. Roy Fitzgerald sitting?"

Dumbfounded, Rock ambled his way up on stage while thousands of home viewers watched Rock's past brought back in the form of several guests from his life in Hollywood and Illinois. Among the guests on the show were agent Henry Willson, actress Piper

Laurie, boyhood friend Edward Jenner, U-I trainer Frankie Van, Mrs. Augdahl (a woman on his Winnetka mail route), his mother (by now Mrs. Joe Olson), high-school classmate James Matteoni, high-school girlfriend Nancy Gillogly, and his aunt on his father's side of the family.

As part of her remembrance, Mrs. Augdahl told how she always used to ask young Roy Fitzgerald in for coffee and a donut. On the television show, she presented Rock with a donut that she brought all the way from Winnetka on the plane. Flabbergasted by the thought, Rock took a bite of the donut and sentimental tears came to his eyes, and he was unable to speak for a few moments. Several fans wrote touching letters to the show, saying how they were impressed by Rock's sincerity. Rock was later to confess, "I hate to disillusion them, but the truth is, one of my pals from Illinois presented me with a donut like I used to go for. While wolfing it down, I got choked. Those tears weren't sentiment . . . just strangulation!"

Filmed in 1952, before his new contract, *Seminole* was Hudson's first 1953 release. In this colorful adventure film about Chief Osceola of the Seminole Indian tribe of the Florida Everglades and the United States Cavalry's aggressive dealings with the tribe in 1835, Rock starred as Lance Caldwell, Osceola's boyhood friend who attempts to intercede between his ambitious commanding officer and Osceola's tribe. The casting alone makes this an entertaining, yet slightly contrived flick. If you can believe Anthony Quinn as Chief Osceola, you can believe anything in this movie. Directed by Budd Boetticher, the cast also includes Barbara Hale, Lee Marvin, and Hugh O'Brien as an Indian named Kajeck who wears his hair in an outrageous red Mohawk.

Next it was off to England where Rock filmed *Sea*

Devils with Yvonne De Carlo. This was the first of his two "loan-out" films that year for Raoul Walsh. The movie was shot on locations in England, on the Channel Islands, and on the French seacoast. Based on Victor Hugo's novel *Toilers of the Sea,* the film was a bawdy "B" movie adventure, complete with bar-room brawls, romance, and intrigue. Yvonne is a French spy and Rock is a smuggler at the time of the French Revolution. They banter back and forth throughout the action. At one point Rock turns to Yvonne and announces, "You're lucky I don't throw you overboard!"

Rock spent a couple of scenes tied up and with his shirt off. In one of these bondage scenes, Yvonne visits Rock and is wearing a low-cut shoulderless dress that exposes half her chest. In the close-up shots, all you can see are the couple's exposed chests and backs, giving the impression that they are both stark naked. Trick photography notwithstanding, this was very steamy stuff indeed. Rock truly earned his title as "beefcake king" in this flick.

Looking back on *Sea Devils,* he was later to comment, "It was a very inexpensive production, so they kept cutting corners to meet the budget to the point where it didn't anywhere match *Toilers of the Sea.* I wasn't too happy about it at the time, but ultimately it doesn't matter."

Naturally, everyone was busy speculating about Rock's offscreen relationship with Yvonne, as this was the fourth (and final) film that they appeared in together. Explained Hudson, "I wasn't used to playing leading parts at that time, nor was I used to the responsibility, and she was quite a star, so there was an adjustment to make. Had I had more experience, I would have been able to get to know her better; she was difficult to get to know—for me. At the time

I didn't know how to get to know anyone, either, so it's probably more my fault than hers."

In other words, anything romantic that existed between them offscreen occurred only in the minds of wishful-thinking fans. It has been theorized that Rock's awkwardness with women during this era of his life eventually led to his initial sexual experiences with other men.

While in England, during the filming of *Sea Devils*, Hudson appeared on the BBC radio network, and thoroughly enjoyed his first taste of foreign-location filming.

Rock's second 1953 film "loan-out" to Raoul Walsh was *Gun Fury*, which costarred Donna Reed as his beautiful fiancée. When she is kidnapped, Rock seeks revenge on her captors. *Gun Fury* was filmed on location in Arizona and was originally released in 3-D.

The Golden Blade (1953) was Rock's twenty-third film, and the first one to be produced as part of his new seven-year contract back at Universal-International. This was his second film opposite Piper Laurie, but unlike *Has Anybody Seen My Gal?* this time around Rock received top billing. The plot of *The Golden Blade* has Rock swashbuckling his way through Old Baghdad—on the Universal back lot. Piper plays the princess in distress, and Rock rescues her with his magic sword.

Back to God's Country (1953) is a remake of a 1927 film by the same name. Rock's leading lady in this one is Marcia Henderson. Hudson and Henderson play a husband and wife fur-trading duo who want to journey down from Canada in a boat with their prize pelts. They are bound for Seattle, but a scoundrel played by Steve Cochran alters their plans, and his dastardly buddy (Hugh O'Brien) is responsible for Rock's breaking his leg. Marcia has to strap Rock to a dogsled and mush those huskies toward their destination.

Next on the program for Rock was a movie that was to become known as his least favorite flick and was constantly to be the butt of jokes. The film found Rock playing the title role of *Taza, Son of Cochise* (1954). Meant to be the sequel to the 1950 film *Broken Arrow, Taza, Son of Cochise* opens with Jeff Chandler reprising his role of the warrior Cochise—who quickly dies, leaving his legacy to son Taza. "I looked like Joe College with a long wig and dark makeup: it was ridiculous!" Rock later commented and laughed. Shot on location in Moab, Utah, this was Hudson's second and last film originally shot and released in 3-D, and his second and last role as an Indian brave.

Looking back on his resistance to playing Taza, Rock explained, "I was under contract, and therefore I had an obligation. But I knew I didn't look right for it. Indians, Mexicans, the Eskimo, they're all really the same race with a similar semi-Oriental appearance. I'm too English looking. Furthermore, I'm too tall. The fact that you make up darker and wear a wig doesn't help you to resemble an Indian. I couldn't even keep my wig on! It kept blowing off in the wind when I rode horseback! An actor takes a role, and an audience either accepts it or rejects it."

After signing his new Universal-International contract and following his two Raoul Walsh "loan-out" films, Rock had returned to the studio for three consecutive "B" adventure films, all without any major success. Although he was a hot screen property, Universal didn't seem to know exactly what to do with him. He had appeared in twenty-five feature films to date—starring in his last seven features. Yet he was not attaining the mega-success that had been predicted for him at this point in his career.

Taza, Son of Cochise was significant for another

reason—it was his second film to be directed by Douglas Sirk, and his first time working for producer Ross Hunter. Together, and separately, Sirk and Hunter were involved in eleven of Hudson's sixty-five feature films.

At Universal studios in 1954, Sirk and Hunter were preparing to do a contemporary melodrama that was to mark a new high point in soap-opera cinema. The film they were readying was *Magnificent Obsession* (1954), and it was to become known as THE movie that made Rock Hudson a star.

"I'm not only going to show you the
town, I'm going to show the town
you."

—Rock Hudson
to Jane Wyman
in *Magnificent Obses-
sion* (1954)

★ 4 ★
THE MATINEE IDOL
1954–1959

MAGNIFICENT OBSESSION was originally a 1935
film starring Irene Dunne and Robert Taylor. In
1953, Ross Hunter and Douglas Sirk had signed
Oscar-winning actress Jane Wyman for a lavish color
remake of the melodrama. Part of her agreement
was the final say as to who her leading man was
going to be.

Sirk and Hunter were interested in Rock Hudson
for the film, but first he had to demonstrate that he
was ready for this major career advancement. He
underwent two days of screen testing on eight different scenes, convincing the producing and directing
duo that he could indeed handle all of the emotional
changes that his character would go through on the
screen. The romantic melodrama represented a vast
departure for Rock from his one-dimensional adventure-film past.

The option was now Jane Wyman's. A well-respected
actress since she won an Oscar for *Johnny Belinda*
(1948), her compatibility with her new leading man
was an important part of her choice. At the time,
Wyman was not familiar with Rock Hudson's films,

so she screened his first starring vehicle, *The Lawless Breed*, and decided that he would be perfect for the role of wealthy and spoiled Bob Merrick.

The production of *Magnificent Obsession* was to commence right after Labor Day in 1953. Rock was all set to begin work on the film that was to represent the biggest break of his career—when he had an accident and ended up in the hospital.

As Rock later recounted, "I broke my collarbone surfing at Laguna Beach two weeks before shooting began. I was too old to cry, but I had the shakes. They gave me a shot to ride to the studio from Laguna Beach in an ambulance, borne on the wings of novocaine, with the police sirens wailing; everybody looked in to see who's there; I waved to them and pretended I was in great agony. I had my shoulder put into a cast at a hospital in the San Fernando Valley and lay flat on my back for a week. I couldn't turn over. I nearly went crazy. Finally, I told the doctor, 'I can't stand this.' He said, 'If you're careful, I'll take it off.' I said, 'Fine!' I had a picture to make, broken bone or no broken bone, and I did the picture with the two ends of the bone still loose. Sometimes they ground together. Jane Wyman, who played the female lead opposite me, always seemed to have her right ear right above the break when the grating noise was going on."

Ironically, in the beginning of *Magnificent Obsession,* Rock's character, careless millionaire playboy Bob Merrick, crashes up his hydrofoil speedboat and ends up in the local hospital. The police have to borrow a tank of oxygen from the local doctor, who is married to Helen Phillips (Jane Wyman). The doctor has a heart attack, and without his only oxygen tank, he dies, leaving Helen a widow. Bob Merrick is an independently wealthy medical school dropout, and he remains alive while dedicated Dr. Phillips is dead.

Bob falls in love with Helen, but she is repelled by him. He pursues her into a cab, and as she escapes through the other car door, she is hit by another automobile and ends up losing her eyesight. Bob falls more deeply in love with the now-blind Helen, and he pretends to be someone else named Robby, whom she falls in love with, not realizing that it is Bob. In the end, Bob is so guilt-ridden and in love that he gets his act together, finishes medical school— and restores Helen's eyesight!

Rock made the transformation from self-centered hedonist Bob Merrick to dedicated Dr. Bob Merrick believable and even appealing. This was also the first film to feature lingering close-ups of Rock, with him staring mesmerizingly into the audience's eyes. "This is the toughest, most complex characterization I've ever attempted," Rock admitted in *Photoplay* magazine while engaged in production of the film.

There was of course the much-demanded scene where Rock got to show off his partially unclothed torso. Hudson defensively explained, "A strange thing happened regarding 'cheesecake' in *Magnificent Obsession*. In researching details of hospital routine, we learned that doctors don't wear shirts under their operating smocks, so in a scene where I'm preparing to operate, I appear nude to the waist. During previews of the picture, the audience hissed, assuming I was trying to show off my chest."

When the film premiered, Louella Parsons asked Rock about the gala opening, inquiring about whom he attended it with. "I took Betty Abbott, the script girl on the picture," he answered. "She has been a friend of mine a long time, and I didn't see why I should take some glamour girl, just for the publicity. My mother and my stepfather Joe went with us. It was my mother's first evening gown, and Joe wore a rented tux. Mom and I have always been very close, and when I asked her if she would talk on the radio at the premiere, she said, 'Oh, yes, indeed . . . I want to.' But when we got up to the theater, with all the lights, the crowds, and the excitement, Mom got cold feet. It was her first premiere."

When Parsons persisted about Rock marrying Betty, Hudson brushed the subject aside by explaining, "I don't honestly know. I have to work on my career and get somewhere. Then it could be. My mother likes Betty and she has been very good for me. We all went out to dinner after the premiere."

When he began work on the film, Rock had expressed his doubts about his contribution to the success of the movie. "When you think about Jane Wyman, Agnes Moorehead . . . what can I possibly contribute to a cast like that?" he publicly asked. "Box-office appeal," that's what he added to the film's success. *Magnificent Obsession* grossed $5.2 million, and Rock's fan mail jumped to a weekly total at the studio of 2700 cards and letters a week. The screen love story of young muscular Rock Hudson romancing an older woman thrilled matinee audiences and made the film one of the year's biggest hits. Jane Wyman received an Academy Award nomination for her performance.

Aside from the publicity and fame that came from the movie, Rock was also winning the respect of his coworkers as well. Jane Wyman became his biggest fan and reported that, "After working with Rock Hudson, I say he's got to be the biggest thing to hit the industry. *Magnificent Obsession* is a wonderful showcase for a new actor. With all the help and cooperation Rock has had, and all the people who want him to be good, he can't help but become one of the big stars in Hollywood, and a moneymaking star at the box office!

"It all adds up to talent, combined with a point of

view and determination," Wyman continued. "If an actor like Rock wants so much to succeed and will work and sustain his courage in the face of rebuffs and disappointments, if he is given the best possible coaching, and if he is fortunate in being assigned roles that will give him the necessary experience, he will reach the top. Rock is not a hipster. He is quiet and possesses within himself a depth of maturity. His attitude is one of study, of developing his mind and his talents by an assiduous study of the best actors and writers, and of reading at great length, to enable him not only to understand his roles, but to be able to communicate them to an audience with complete realism."

Rock loved working with Jane Wyman as much as she liked having him as her costar. "I don't think anyone ever thought I'd do anything important until I was given the wonderfully spiritual story *Magnificent Obsession,* with Jane Wyman. What a wonderful girl Jane is. She helped me a lot. You know, she calls me the 'Great White Hope'!"

Rock knew that *Magnificent Obsession* was going to be the most important film in his career at that point. The knowledge came "one night at a sneak preview. It was at the Encino Theater. And I fled the theater before the film was over. I knew . . . KNEW! And I knew I had to get out of there before the lights went on . . . and I was emotional," Rock recalled.

Hudson confessed that his newfound success changed the way people looked at him. He was no longer an aspiring star . . . he was a bona-fide movie star at last, and many people tried to draw him into their social circles. Said Rock, "After the premiere, people suddenly began to take notice of me, they began to invite me out for meals. And I'd go. Suddenly I found I was getting involved with people I disliked and spending time at parties being bored to death."

Modern Screen magazine awarded Rock Hudson the title of "Most Popular Actor of 1954." *Photoplay* heralded his *Magnificent Obsession* performance one of 1954's five best screen portrayals. And *Look* magazine proclaimed Rock the "Top Male Movie Star of 1955," based on his box-office magnetism.

Although he was suddenly a big-time movie star, Rock's next two movie assignments found him back in the "Grade B" adventure mold.

His twenty-seventh feature film, *Bengal Brigade* (1954), found him opposite Arlene Dahl. Rock is in India as a British officer with the Bengal troops in the 1850s. For *Captain Lightfoot* (1955), Rock starred with Barbara Rush in a tale of rebellion in Ireland. Unlike the back-lot look of *Bengal Brigade, Captain Lightfoot* was beautifully filmed on location in Ireland, produced by Ross Hunter, and directed by Douglas Sirk. In the film, Hudson portrays a Robin Hood of the Emerald Isle. Before he joined the company on location, Rock traveled to France, Italy, England, and Scandinavia.

It was back to the soap-opera format for Rock's next movie, *One Desire*. Based on the novel *Tacey Cromwell,* Hudson portrayed gambler Clint Saunders to Anne Baxter's social climber Tacey. During the course of the action, Clint and Tacey adopt an orphan girl named Seely, who is played by young Natalie Wood.

A year and a half after the box-office smash *Magnificent Obsession* was released, Universal reunited Rock Hudson with Jane Wyman for *All That Heaven Allows* (1955). Again Hunter and Sirk were the producing/directing team, and again Agnes Moorhead costarred.

This time around Jane played widow Cary Scott,

who falls in love with the young man who works on the trees and shrubs in her yard in the well-manicured suburbs. As Ron Kirby, Rock pours on the charm with his enticingly uncomplicated life-style. Cary is immediately attracted to Ron's unpretentious manner and feels alive for the first time since her husband's death.

Two major factors complicate their May/September romance. First, Cary's spoiled teenage children are embarrassed and humiliated by the affair between their mom and a much younger man. Second, the town is peopled by petty, gossiping society women who have Cary married off to the dapper but dull bachelor Harvey. Over forty, he reminds Cary's college-age children of the father they are missing. Cary tries unsuccessfully to put her happiness aside for the sake of public opinion. Just as she is about to rekindle her romance with Ron, he falls off a cliff and goes into a coma. This time around it's up to Jane to nurse Rock back to health. With all of the melodramatic appeal of their first movie, *All That Heaven Allows* enjoyed similar box-office success.

Rock was suddenly one of the hottest subjects in the fan magazines. He recalled, "A favorite question among fan magazines was whether I slept in the nude. I couldn't understand who could give a damn about my sleeping habits . . . I went through a great deal of learning to sleep in the nude. From my childhood, I remembered my mother saying, 'Well, if there's a fire . . .' and I thought, right indeed, what if there's a fire—I'd have to run out naked. Then when I was twenty-one, I thought, 'Hell, if there's a fire you can just wrap a blanket around you.' And I've slept in the nude ever since."

In 1954, Rock made a guest appearance on *The Jack Benny Show* on television, and in 1955 he appeared on *I Love Lucy* with Lucille Ball and

Desi Arnez. In a fan magazine called *Hollywood Diary*, Rock wrote as a diary entry for March 9, 1955: "Reported to the Motion Picture Center for the advance filming on *I Love Lucy*. Still can't get used to Desi, who insists on calling me 'Rook.' I also can't get used to the three TV cameras that are going simultaneously and the live audience; it seems strange after a scene to hear applause. Television, huh?"

At the time, Rock's strongest relationship was with his mother, Mrs. Kay Olsen. According to Rock in 1953, "My mother is a telephone operator. I don't like for her to work, but she won't quit. Says she just loves to talk. She tells everybody about me. My publicity has gone to her head."

According to Kay in 1954, Rock's success hadn't gone to *his* head at all, in fact she had watched her son become warmer, more relaxed with himself, and more giving. She explained, "Not that Rock hasn't been kind and considerate before, only until now, he has never been able to show or express his feelings in any way, even to me. Yet he hasn't developed, and I don't believe he ever will, into the handshaking 'Glad to see you, what did you say your name was?' kind of person. That's partly because he dislikes small talk, partly because he hasn't completely outgrown a shyness, particularly toward women. This is also one of the reasons why most of his dates are connected with the film industry and usually from his own studio."

Kay recounted that when Rock was in the navy he mailed forty dollars from the Philippines to his mother, instructing her to buy herself a dress and to spend the rest for flowers for a girl named Nancy, who lived in Winnetka. She complied, and two weeks later received a note from Rock which read, "Mother, you sent the flowers to the wrong Nancy!" She simply replied, "That's what you get for not telling me more about your girls. How should I know which one you meant?"

Kay also observed at this time, "Rock has the wonderful ability of not only getting a tremendous enjoyment out of giving, but does it without expecting anything in return. This way he has never been, and probably never will be, disappointed in people."

Citing an example, Kay observed that according to her son, "An elderly fellow who works at the studio—we call him Pop Schroeder—had a heart attack a few days ago." He then inquired about some leftover turkey from their Christmas dinner, adding that, "I thought I'd stop by on my way home and take it to him. I'd like to wish him a happy Christmas, anyhow." Kay was surprised and impressed by Rock's gesture.

Since he was becoming so successful, Rock was getting quite generous with his gifts. At Christmas he told his mother, "I won't beat around the bush, Mom. You have your choice between a deep freeze, a dishwasher, and an automatic washing machine. Which one would you prefer?"

Said Kay, "After much deliberation, I decided on a washing machine. Imagine my surprise when in addition, he also gave me a matching dryer!" According to her, his logic was that he "thought I'd save you some steps so you can conserve your strength to cook dinner when I come over!"

When she was visiting her son one day, she commented that she loved the cup of coffee that he had just made her. With that he insisted that his new coffeemaker, which had produced the prized brew, was now a present for her . . . and he gave it to her on the spot.

Rock's next film was *Never Say Goodbye* (1956), a remake of the 1945 Merle Oberon and Charles Korvin movie, *This Love of Ours*. Rock played Dr. Michael

Parker, who suspects his wife Lisa (Cornell Borchers) of adultery and leaves her, only to find out that he was wrong.

Written on the Wind (1956) was Rock's thirty-second film and is a camp classic. Rock plays Mitch Wayne, whose best friend is millionaire Kyle Hadley (Robert Stack). Kyle's sister Marylee (Dorothy Malone) falls for Mitch, but he isn't interested. Kyle falls in love with Lucy Moore (Lauren Bacall), to whom Mitch is also attracted. When Lucy discloses that she is pregnant, Kyle suspects that Mitch is the baby's father. In the end, the distraught Kyle shoots himself, and Marylee becomes the town whore to get even with Mitch for not loving her. As slutty Marylee, Malone won the "Best Supporting Actress" Academy Award while Robert Stack also received a nomination for his role. The film grossed $4.4 million, and only further added to Rock's now-established box-office appeal.

Rock's next film was the award-winning epic *Giant* (1956). Along with *Magnificent Obsession* and *Pillow Talk*, *Giant* provided Hudson with one of the three most famous roles of his entire career: Bick Benedict.

In 1955, when it was announced that producer/director George Stevens was about to mount a mammoth production of *Giant* based on the best-selling novel by Edna Ferber, all of Hollywood was anxious to be involved in the film. *Giant* was intended to be to the Texas oil empires what *Gone with the Wind* was to the Civil War.

At this point, Rock Hudson was such a hot property that he was busily hustled from one movie set to another in an effort to utilize him in as many productions as possible. Although *Giant* was filmed in 1955 and released in 1956, it was shot after two of Rock's 1957 releases: *Battle Hymn* and *Something of Value*. According to Rock, "There was one day between the finish of *Something of Value* and the beginning of *Giant*. I'd had no chance to talk to George Stevens, who was directing *Giant*. I'd been studying a Texan accent for months, but I hadn't had a chance to study him [Stevens]. I didn't know what he wanted from me; so I called him up and said that I was nervous, that I didn't know what he wanted me to do or how he wanted me to do it. Working for Stevens is scary. He's a perfectionist. There was also the angle of my playing opposite Elizabeth Taylor too, which made me jumpy. She was already so big in her own right."

He further explained, "Stevens said a wonderful thing. He said, 'Why don't you just come in to work anyhow, and we'll see what we can do. I'm worried about this picture too, Rock.' That calmed me. He's hypnotic. He puts the whammy on you and after that you feel you've got to do what he tells you to do. Stevens has never claimed that he's 'made' an actor or an actress. If you're as big as Stevens, you don't need to wear braces on your ego."

The casting for *Giant* went through many changes. Originally, Stevens had wanted to cast Grace Kelly in the role of Leslie Benedict. The film spanned the lives of the Benedict family from the 1930s to the 1950s, and in a very literal sense was the precursor of the television series *Dallas*. Elizabeth Taylor was waiting for a film role that had the scope, character development, and fire that Leslie Benedict possessed. She begged her studio, M-G-M, to loan her out to Stevens's production of *Giant* which was being done at Warner Brothers. Much to her delight, she was made available by M-G-M, with full knowledge of what this could do for her box-office appeal when she returned. Likewise, Universal-International was willing to loan out Rock Hudson to Warner Brothers for the role of Bick Benedict, fully aware of what kind of prestige this would bring to his career. Oddly enough, there was also talk about Clark Gable, William Holden, or Gary Cooper being cast as Bick strictly for their box-office appeal, but their portrayal of young Bick would have required altering for a more mature actor.

For the role of Jett Rink, Stevens cast one of the hottest young actors in Hollywood: James Dean. This would be Dean's crowning achievement, having just become the rage of teenage moviegoers via his huge successes in *Rebel Without a Cause* (1955) and *East of Eden* (1955).

With Elizabeth Taylor, Rock Hudson, and James Dean all signed for the lead roles in *Giant*, Stevens was assured that his epic film was going to have the proper magnitude that he intended for it to possess. The huge cast also included Mercedes McCambridge, Jane Withers, Chill Wills, Dennis Hopper, Rod Taylor (billed as Rodney Taylor), Sal Mineo, Earl Holliman, and in her first film role, Carroll Baker.

Everything about the film version of *Giant* (1956) is of epic dimentions, from Dimitri Tiomkin's musical score to William C. Mellor's cinematography. The film begins in the 1930s when Bick Benedict (Rock Hudson) travels north to Maryland to see a prize horse that he is interested in purchasing. Along with his sister, Benedict has inherited his Texas family's ranch, Reata. He meets and falls in love with the wealthy horse breeder's daughter, Leslie Clinch (Elizabeth Taylor), whom he promptly marries.

Since his parents have died, Bick and his mannish sister Luz (Mercedes McCambridge) run Reata. When Bick returns to his Texas cattle ranch with his feminine and headstrong new wife, sparks fly between the two women.

Bick finds that in his absence, Luz has hired her friend, and Bick's rival, to help out at Reata: Jett Rink (James Dean). So, upon their Texas reunion, both Bick's and Luz's egos are immediately threatened by their same-sex rivals.

When Luz suddenly dies in an accident, she leaves Jett a strip of land in her will, which Bick tries unsuccessfully to con Jett out of. Bick is jealous of Leslie's budding friendship with Jett, knowing that Jett is in love with Leslie, even though she is the mother of Bick's children. When Jett strikes oil on the strip of land that Luz has left him, he becomes the wealthiest man in the country, and the Texas rivalry is in full swing.

Not to be outdone, Bick chucks the cattle business and successfully drills for oil. When Bick and Leslie's children grow up, Jett is attracted to their fiery daughter Luz II (Carroll Baker) since he can't have Leslie.

The three-hour-and-eighteen-minute mega-movie is filled with love, hate, prejudice, intrigue, and the type of dynamic character development that made it one of the most highly praised and respected achievements in each of the three principal stars' careers.

As the filming of *Giant* spanned the spring and summer of 1955, Rock Hudson and company knew that the film that they were working on was going to be a hit, and many lasting friendships developed on the set. Both Elizabeth Taylor and Jane Withers were to become lifelong friends of Rock's, and both former child actresses were to be supportive of Hudson when he became ill in 1985.

According to George Stevens, Rock demonstrated the kind of acting skill that earmarked him for lasting career success. Said Stevens at the time, "Right now Hudson is a better actor than Gable was in *Gone with the Wind*. Right now, he's a good as [Gregory] Peck or [Humphrey] Bogart. Of course, he's not Freddie [Fredric] March yet ... but he may be in time!"

In several scenes, Stevens wanted to make sure

that Rock had a very commanding appearance, especially when it came to his height. On June 28, 1955, Hudson reported, "Liz and I played our first love scene today. I was amazed when Stevens handed me a box and said, 'Stand on it.' Usually they dig a trench and put me in it so I'll shrink closer to the leading lady's height. He wants to point up the difference. When I picked Liz up and kissed her, her feet dangled so far from the ground that her shoes fell off!"

Hudson also spoke of the hardship of shooting the film in the Texas heat. "It's powerful hot in Marfa, Texas. Better get used to it, for we'll be here two weeks. Only relaxation is when Liz Taylor, Jimmy Dean, and I drive to the next town for a swim."

He claimed that he loved working with Elizabeth, and told one reporter, "I'm crazy about her. She's the only woman I've ever known who makes me dizzy. I used to ask her, 'How can you sit there being so beautiful?' and she'd say, 'Knock it off, will you?' Then she'd point out what she felt was wrong with her looks and I'd be staring, growing limper and limper. What a woman!"

According to Rock, one of his most difficult scenes in *Giant* was the one that took place at the dinner table at the Clinch house in Maryland. In it he had to concentrate on his facial expressions, because much of the action is played off of his reactions to the conversation. He is required to let the audience know that he is fascinated and deeply in love with Leslie (Elizabeth) in a subtle and nonverbal way. He explained, "The dinner-table scene was a stickler. I knew a lot depended on me in that one, and I was stiff as a board. So George [Stevens] shot the master and everyone else's coverage first, then instead of bringing a camera in close to me, he sat me in a chair with lights all around, put the camera way off with a magnifying lens, and said he wanted a line rehearsal—just to see how it would come out. Since I thought it was just a rehearsal, I relaxed. But he was rolling—and got what he wanted. How often do you find a director like that?"

Looking back on that film, Rock had even more praise for Stevens. "*Giant* won him the directing Oscar that year, and he deserved it. Stevens was one of the all-time greats, and he had me doing things I never thought I could do. He got me to do scenes his way—and made me think it was my idea. If nothing else, he could trick you into a performance."

The makeup that was utilized to age each of the characters during the thirty-year span of the film was crucial to its success with the audience. Said Hudson, "Have you ever wondered what you'd look like in thirty years? It's pretty frightening when those Warners makeup boys working on *Giant* get ahold of you and turn you into a sixty-year-old man in one afternoon. I ended up with a potbelly, furrowed brow, and gray hair. After sitting in the makeup chair for three hours looking at my reflection in the mirror, I thought, 'Better go on a diet, young feller! ' "

It was exactly thirty years later that the world was shocked by Rock's appearance in the summer of 1985. Hudson was never to be able to look into the mirror and see what he would look like at sixty, as he died one and one half months before his sixtieth birthday.

By mid-September of 1955, the *Giant* company had completed their location photography and had been doing interiors back in the studio in Hollywood. The filming was almost completed, and on September 26, 1955, James Dean had finished his final scene on the picture and had returned to his notoriously wild life-style. Four days later, he was speeding his silver Porsche Spyder through the streets near Paso Robles, California, when he smashed head-on into the side of another car and was killed.

"I can't believe it, George; I can't believe it!" said a shocked Elizabeth Taylor when Stevens telephoned her with the news. "I just can't believe this awful thing has happened. Not to Jimmy—he was so young, so full of life." Liz reportedly cried the whole night long, and the next morning Stevens called her and told her to report to the set to finish her final scene in *Giant*. She never forgave him for that.

Rock was later to say that "George was not very kind to her. Elizabeth is very extreme in her likes and dislikes. If she likes, she loves. If she doesn't like, she loathes. And she has a temper, an incredible temper which she loses at any injustice. George forced her to come to work after Dean's death. He hadn't finished the film. And she could not stop crying. Remember that scene in my office? She kept sobbing and sobbing, so he photographed me over the back of her head. But she let him have it."

"I hope you rot in Hell!" Liz screamed at Stevens as she stormed off the set that day. The film was completed two weeks later when Liz had gotten over her anger.

The finished product was one of the finest films that Hollywood produced in the 1950s, and when it was released in videocassette in 1985, *Giant* again became a smash. In theatrical release alone, the film made $14 million, and when the Academy Award nominations were announced in early 1957, Rock Hudson and James Dean were up for the "Best Actor" award, Mercedes McCambridge was nominated as "Best Supporting Actress," George Stevens was nominated as "Best Director," and the film itself was up for "Best Production." In the end, only Stevens was to win the Oscar statuette. In the "Best Actor" category, the winner was Yul Brenner for *The King and I,* beating Kirk Douglas in *Lust for Life,* and Laurence Olivier in *Richard III,* as well as Hudson and Dean.

Rock never forgot his confusion at the Manhattan premiere of *Giant.* He was to explain, "A terribly unnerving thing happened to me when it was premiered in New York. It was the first time a movie I was in was ever premiered. So I was impressed—thrilled. Outside the theater were thousands of people. Traffic was blocked. All of that. And I thought, 'My God, *I'm* in this movie, playing one of the leads!' Jesus, it was exciting. Then I sat there in my seat—and I was 'booed' throughout the film! Luckily I wasn't sitting on the aisle, because if I had been, I would have gotten up and left! The 'booing' was quite vociferous. It was terrifying. And it wasn't until the fight near the end of the film—where the bigot I was playing was tangling with a worse bigot and getting a couple of good licks on him—that suddenly I was applauded. And it was only then that I realized that the audience was reacting so volubly to the character. Not to me . . . but to Bick!"

Rock's thirty-fourth film was the entertaining tale *Four Girls in Town* (1956), about four star-struck girls who arrive at Universal Studios in Hollywood. In the film Rock has a brief part as himself. The girls were played by Julie Adams, Marianne Cook, Elsa Martinelli, and Gia Scala. The male lead in the film was a new actor by the name of George Nader.

George Nader was born in Los Angeles in 1921 and decided to pursue an acting career. He was reportedly "discovered" in a theater production at the Pasadena Playhouse by actress Jeanne Crain. She was about to star in the campus drama entitled *Take Care of My Little Girl* (1951) and was responsible for his joining Mitzi Gaynor, Dale Robertson, Jeffrey Hunter, Jean Peters, and herself in the film. In 1954,

Nader was one of Anne Baxter's costars in *Carnival Story,* and the following year he was Maureen O'Hara's leading man in *Lady Godiva.* Around the time of the filming of *Four Girls in Town,* Rock became friendly with George.

Confidential magazine was one of the most controversial publications of the 1950s. With rampant McCarthyism blazing through America at the time, *Confidential* fit right in with the witch-hunting atmosphere. The magazine thrived on good juicy Hollywood scandal and finally went bankrupt in a sea of inevitable lawsuits. However, when it was in full swing, the magazine was famous for printing stories about who was sleeping with whom in Hollywood. Among its juicier features were cover stories like "Why Liberace's Theme Song Should Be 'Mad About the Boy'" and "The Night Lana Turner and Ava Gardner Shared a Lover!"

Confidential was looking for blood when it discovered in 1955 that Rock Hudson was gay. Now there was a cover story that was sure to sell magazines! Henry Willson was livid when he found that *Confidential* was planning to print a story about how Rock's magnificent obsession wasn't for young starlets. Universal-International executives were quite shaken about the prospect of blowing the fortune they had invested in Rock's stardom and his all-American he-man image. Everything would be lost if they didn't think fast.

According to a 1985 article that appeared in *People* magazine, "The studio cut a deal that traded information on Rock for information about a lesser-known actor who was gay." In a subsequent article, *People* identified the actor as George Nader. *Confidential* went ahead and published the story about Nader, and George was finished in the movies. In 1985, when Rock Hudson's will was disclosed following his death, the bulk of his estate went to George Nader.

Rock had just narrowly escaped a brush with career disaster, but that wasn't any insurance that *Confidential* still wasn't going to make an attempt to ruin his stardom with public details about his sex life. It was Henry Willson who decided that Rock had to get married . . . immediately. All they needed was a bride. Willson's secretary Phyllis Gates was the right age, and she was available. Would she consider suddenly marrying Rock Hudson? Of course . . . what available girl on the planet wouldn't want to suddenly become Mrs. Rock Hudson?

As recently as October 3, 1955, *Life* magazine had carried a cover story on Rock Hudson entitled "Hollywood's Most Handsome Bachelor." Yet on November 9, 1955, Hudson suddenly eloped with Phyllis, and they were wed in a bungalow at the Santa Barbara Biltmore Hotel. The ceremony was performed by Reverend Nordahl B. Thorpe, a minister at the Trinity Lutheran Church of Santa Barbara. The maid of honor was a friend of Phyllis's named Pat Devlin, and the best man was Rock's boyhood friend James Matteoni.

According to Matteoni, "We met Phyllis for the first time when he was going to marry her. Roy called up at two in the morning and said, 'I've made arrangements for you to be on a six o'clock flight. Keep it a secret.' We went to a courthouse two or three minutes before it closed—so that the reporters had already left. Then we went to a hotel where a cottage suite had been taken. After the ceremony, we each had to call one of the columnists to let them all know at the same time." After that the wedding party left for a restaurant called Talk of the Town.

Phyllis and Rock honeymooned in Bermuda and moved into his small two-bedroom Hollywood bachelor pad. For a while he played the happy married man for the press, but he soon grew to regret the camouflage marriage. Trying to make the best of her situation, Phyllis reportedly attempted to seduce Rock by dressing in skimpy nightgowns, but Rock was clearly not interested in her or their marriage.

His former leading lady Arlene Dahl later confirmed that his close Hollywood friends knew that "Phyllis was not the love of his life. It was an arrangement." Likewise, actress Mamie Van Doren admitted that she had gone on studio-arranged dates with Rock, and confirmed, "We all knew Rock was gay, but it never made any difference to us. Universal invested a lot of money in Rock, and it was important for his image to remain that of a lady-killer." Of the marriage, Van Doren explained, "Rock did what was expected of him."

However, just like the fabricated stories about his wrecking the navy plane and being "discovered" delivering his résumé to Henry Willson, Rock obligingly supplied magazine writers with stories about his blissful life with his new bride. In the March 1957 issue of *McCall's*, he gushed, "We live like any other young married couple. So, it's hard to get used to the lack of privacy in my life. When I bought Phyllis's engagement ring, a columnist printed the number of carats of the diamonds and how much it cost. A few months ago I bought Phyllis a mink stole for a birthday surprise. Two days later a Hollywood column told all about the present and my surprise went out the window." He also talked about how he and Phyllis "dream of having a houseful of children."

It finally got to the point where Rock was sick of living his life for the benefit of the press. According to Rock, "I had been married only a few weeks when one fan-magazine writer came on a movie set where I was working and asked, 'What do you and your wife do at night?' 'I beg your pardon?' I said. But this fan-mag writer kept at it so I said sarcastically,

'Look, I have my wife take all her clothes off and dance on the coffee table for me!' "

With stories like that in print, anything that *Confidential* or any other scandal magazine could print could be dismissed as "vicious rumors." Rock's reputation was once again safe, and Phyllis had to go.

By 1958 the marriage had served its purpose, and on August 3 of that year, on the grounds of "extreme cruelty," Phyllis was granted a divorce. She finally realized that the marriage was hopeless, and Rock couldn't wait to get out of it. Phyllis testified in court that "He was sullen and would not talk to me for weeks at a time. Sometimes he would stay out all night and when I asked where he had been, he would say, 'It's none of your business.' " Phyllis received a $130,000 cash settlement.

In 1960, after it was all over, a writer for the *Saturday Evening Post* pressured Rock about the fact that "I've read that your marriage was 'made,' not by you but by the same agent who is reported to have made a star of you." Rock replied, "I'm sure you did read that. I read it too, and it made me feel like an idiot. What actually happened was this. My wife was my agent's secretary. I met her in a supermarket. She introduced herself. She told me who she was. Naturally I had talked to her many times on the phone. For a while we had a lot of trouble getting together. Either I had a date or she had one. We went together for a year and were married. But it didn't work out. We stayed married only a couple of years. Last summer our divorce was final. Now I'm single again."

One of Rock's covered-up affairs from this era was with Tyrone Power. To camouflage this news, a cover story was planted in *Modern Screen* implying that it was Power's wife that Rock was interested in. "The romance that is shocking Hollywood . . . ROCK! ARE

YOU GOING TO MARRY DEBBIE?" ran in the June 1959 issue of the magazine.

After his marriage was dissolved, Rock bought a house in Newport Beach in an effort to conduct his personal life out from under the microscope of Hollywood columnists. Said Hudson, "Thank God, my beach home in Newport is not on the route of any of the tourist buses whose driver points out the movie stars' homes. People down there pay no attention to me."

On the evening of May 12, 1956, Elizabeth Taylor and her then-husband Michael Wilding gave a dinner party for several of their close friends. Present were Kevin McCarthy, Montgomery Clift, Eddie Dmytryk (director of *Raintree County*) and his wife Jean, and Rock Hudson and his new bride Phyllis Gates. After the guests had consumed several bottles of red wine, Clift announced that he had already had too much to drink and was ready to leave. He was certain that he could drive himself, but only if his buddy Kevin would help him down the hill. Liz and Michael Wilding lived in one of the mountaintop homes in the Hollywood Hills.

Kevin got into his car and Monty was to follow right behind him, in his own automobile. Monty had taken two "downs" with his wine, and he missed a turn, crashing his car into a utility pole and smashing his face through the windshield. McCarthy sped back to Liz Taylor's for help and the rest of the dinner party followed. Even before the ambulance, the press photographers arrived. Clift's face was a swollen bloody mess, and his front teeth were knocked halfway down his throat.

According to Rock Hudson, "Elizabeth prevented the photographers from taking Monty's picture by the foulest language I have ever heard. She shocked them out of taking it. 'You son of a bitch!' she said.

'I'll kick you in the nuts. If you dare take a picture of him like this, I'll never let you near me again. Get out of here, you fucking bastards!' "

Wilding, McCarthy, and Hudson formed a block to keep the photographers from getting anywhere near Clift. Finally the ambulance arrived and took over, and the paparazzi dispersed in shock. At times like these, Rock was always remembered by his Hollywood pals as a selfless friend in any emergency.

While all of this craziness was going on in Rock's personal life, his image on the movie screen was as strong as ever. Each of his next six films added to his public image of a macho he-man romantic hero. As Lauren Bacall expressed at the time, "You feel Rock when he comes on screen. You're always sure of him, always rooting for him."

Rock's thirty-fifth film was entitled *Battle Hymn* (1957). Produced by Ross Hunter and directed by Douglas Sirk, it was based on the true story of Colonel Dean Hess and his life in combat in World War II and in the Korean War. The film was shot before *Giant* was filmed, but released after *Giant* hit the theaters. Hess was a minister from Ohio when he enlisted in the air force for duty in Korea. When he was in combat in World War II, he had accidently bombed a church, killing thirty-seven innocent children. He carried his guilt to Korea in 1950, and he helped organize an airlift that was dubbed "Operation Kiddie Kar"—in which four hundred war orphans were systematically removed from the arena of combat. Robert Mitchum had asked to be cast as Hess, but Hess protested that he was not going to have his life story brought to life on the screen by an ex-jailbird (referring to Mitchum's late 1940s marijuana bust). Rock was given the role and delivered a convincing and powerful performance.

Something of Value, his next film, was released in

April 1957. Rock had been loaned out to M-G-M for the payment of $400,000 to Universal. The film is set in Kenya and tells the story of two boyhood friends, one black and one white. When they grow up, the black friend, Kimani (Sidney Poitier) can't sit by and watch the social injustices that are happening to his people, and he joins the radical group Mau Mau. The white friend, Peter McKenzie (Rock), is forced to fight the black group when rebellion takes hold. Both men are forced to put aside their boyhood ideals when confronted by the insanity of politics and racism.

Based on his string of recent screen successes, M-G-M offered $750,000 to Universal-International to lend Rock out to them to star in their planned gladiator epic *Ben Hur* (1959). According to Rock, it was his choice not to do the film. "I could have done *Ben Hur*, but I would have had to give the studio [Universal] another year," he said. Charleton Heston took the film and won the "Best Actor" Academy Award for his performance.

Instead, Rock's next film was *The Tarnished Angels* (1957), which reunited him with Robert Stack and Dorothy Malone. Based on a William Faulkner novel, *Pylon*, the action centers around a veteran aviator from World War I (Stack), who is now reduced to a stunt-flying job. He convinces his wife (Malone) to have an affair with someone who can finance the new airplane he needs. A local reporter (Hudson) is in love with the wife, so he devises a way in which Stack can have the plane, and he can have Malone. Unfortunately the plane ends up crashing with Stack in it.

Portraying Burke Devlin, the has-been newspaper reporter, Rock began the film playing Burke as a down-on-his-luck lush—a newsman who hit the bottle harder than his typewriter keys. After two days of camera work, U-I ordered Hudson's already-shot footage to be immediately scrapped and redone. Hudson explained, "In those days it took two days for the dailies to come back for the front office to see. Word shot down. 'Oh, no! You're a leading man, you can't do that!' So we had to go back and reshoot and I had to do the picture wearing a fedora and a press card in the hatband."

Robert Stack has a special memory of Rock on the set of *The Tarnished Angels*. Says Stack, "My wife was about to give birth, and we were on location, stuck in the middle of nowhere. Unbeknownst to me, [Rock] had communication with the hospital. As soon as he found out Elizabeth was born, he had a biplane take off with a banner that said, 'It's a Girl!' I was about four or five miles away, doing a scene with Bob Middleton, and all of a sudden Middleton looked up and said, 'There's some bastard coming right at us.' Right across the set flew this old plane with a banner saying, 'It's a Girl.' " Stack further praised Hudson by stating, "He really is a gentleman, and in this town that's not too easy to be . . . he's such a well-mannered, wonderful guy."

Rock was next scheduled to be directed by Douglas Sirk in *A Time to Love and a Time to Die* (1958). He was offered the "loan-out" film *Sayonara* (1957), but he opted for a third film, *Farewell to Arms* (1957), which was being produced by David O. Selznick for Twenieth Century–Fox. Said Rock, "Now that was a helluva decision to have to make. They were two pretty snappy stories. I went with *A Farewell to Arms* because it was David O. Selznick, who had made the best picture ever made, *Gone with the Wind* (1939)." John Gavin ended up starring in *A Time to Love and a Time to Die,* while Marlon Brando received an Academy Award nomination for *Sayonara* in the part Rock was to play. Although Rock picked the prestige production, the outcome was something of an overproduced dinosaur.

A Farewell to Arms was originally a 1932 film starring Gary Cooper and Helen Hayes. Based on Ernest Hemingway's story about a nurse in love with an ambulance driver during World War I, the novel was later readapted for the screen as a World War II drama in the 1951 film *Force of Arms* starring William Holden and Nancy Olson. It was rumored that the third attempt to film *A Farewell to Arms* grew out of an effort by Selznick to find a suitable film vehicle for his actress-wife Jennifer Jones.

Filmed on location in Italy, *A Farewell to Arms* was besieged with production problems from the very beginning. When the company arrived in Italy, John Houston, who was originally set to direct the film, quit. He was replaced by Charles Vidor. Vidor had two production assistants—Art Fellows and Andrew Marton. Artistic disputes between Selznick and Fellows resulted in at least one altercation, and in other artistic skirmishes, one special-effects director, one film editor, and three art directors quit and stormed off of the set.

It seems that Selznick wanted to have his hands on every aspect of this film and alienated everyone on his production team. It also seems that Rock Hudson was the only member of the company who didn't complain about Selznick during the filming of *A Farewell to Arms*. Rock's dialogue coach, Jim Duncan, was quoted as proclaiming, "I have never heard Rock say anything bad about a soul, living or dead." His reputation for professionalism was one of the characteristics that made Hudson such a popular performer for so many years.

When *A Farewell to Arms* had its premiere in Hollywood on December 17, 1957, its running length was

150 minutes. The critics loved the lingering panoramic shots of the beautiful scenery, but reviews of the performances of Jones and Hudson as the tragically ill-fated lovers were mixed. Hudson was praised for delivering an "earnest" screen portrayal, while Jones decidedly got the "thumbs down" for her stilted one. Mercedes McCambridge was also in the cast of this film, reunited with Rock for the first time since they played brother and sister in *Giant*.

Rock's popularity continued to blossom throughout this period—despite the fact that he had disappointed many of his fans by marrying Phyllis Gates. Crowds had swarmed the streets when Rock received an honorary degree in the spring of 1957 from Marietta College in Marietta, Ohio.

Handsome Hudson's fan mail had reached such proportions (ten thousand a month!) that he had to hire a secretary and to invest the annual sum of $10,000 into his official newsletter, entitled the *Hudson Herald*. The quarterly newsletter contained such regular features as "Idol Thoughts," plus the published love poems of his female worshipers. Included in the contents of the *Hudson Herald* were tips on how to go about corresponding with Rock. His fans were specifically instructed NOT to ask anything about his personal life. The reason given in the newsletter was that "he doesn't like to have to refuse to discuss these things with us!" Understandably so, in retrospect.

After all of the hero worship that was directed toward him, Rock was beginning to relax a bit more with the fact of his fame as a handsome screen sex symbol. "I don't like to talk about I-I-I . . . just once I would like to say how ridiculous I am, not how great," he expressed, pointing out some of his weaknesses: "I think my eyes are dull and uninteresting, a kind of shoe-polish brown. I don't see anything unusual about them." He added, "I chew my nails whenever I get nervous. I chew my nails whenever I see a movie, and when I'm working in one as I am now. I'm always a nervous wreck . . . I suppose it's a better nervous habit than eating too much. Nails grow fast, but weight shows on you, and it doesn't come off very quickly."

On March 26, 1958, Rock was seen by millions of television viewers in the telecast of the thirtieth annual Academy Awards presentations. He was seen singing a duet of "Baby, It's Cold Outside" with one of the true legends of Hollywood: Mae West! Explained Hudson, "That was in the new days of televising the Academy Awards, so they felt that there had to be some form of entertainment involved. You know—mix it up, give an award and then have somebody do something and then have another award presentation. And the show started with a few bars of every song that had ever won an Academy Award— of which 'Baby It's Cold Outside' was one. It was very exciting for the world to see. That had never happened to me before. I was in front of a live audience: that had never happened before. And I was singing: that also had never happened before. Furthermore—there was Mae West!

"Of course, I'd seen her in films since I was a kid. So I was pretty staggered by it all. We went down to her house for rehearsals. We did that for a couple of weeks. And she was always in a sort of pale beige negligee with a train about twenty-feet long. That's how we rehearsed every day. And when we'd stop for a breather, we'd sit and talk. She was just plain and simply a sweet old lady, who told me marvelous stories about her life."

"But," continued Hudson, "the minute we'd start

rehearsing, all of a sudden she was Mae West—giving me all of that thing that she did. She broke me up constantly. Constantly! We never got through the song. And we didn't on the show either. Because she gave me the giggles. She thought that all the sex queens in movie history were a bunch of bullshit. She said if they didn't have a sense of humor with it, it wasn't worthwhile."

After his divorce from Phyllis, Rock temporarily took a house in Malibu before moving south to Newport beach. He bought himself a boat and often took a group of his friends skindiving off of it. One particular day, a Hollywood stuntman named Paul Stater was aboard. Reminiscing on the deck of Rock's boat, Stater recalled that he had once done a screen dive off a boat into a lagoon, as Jon Hall's stunt-man in the Dorothy Lamour film *The Hurricane*. Rock couldn't believe his ears! "You son of a bitch!" he exclaimed, laughing. "It's your fault that I wanted to be an actor; I thought all along it had been Jon Hall!"

Rock's next film was *Twilight for the Gods* (1958), with Cyd Charisse, Arthur Kennedy, and Leif Erickson. Rock portrayed the captain of a tramp steamer bound for Mexico. The passengers' and crew's hopes, fears, and flaws are elaborated when the ship goes down. It was followed by Hudson's fortieth film, *This Earth Is Mine* (1959), set in the wine country of the Napa Valley, in California. His costars were Dorothy McGuire and Claude Rains.

Said Rock of his role in *This Earth Is Mine*, "I play kind of a jerk. In the movie, the head of our family owns the largest vineyard in the world, here in the Napa Valley. Then Prohibition comes. The old man won't sell his grapes to gangsters who want to make wine. He almost goes broke. I make a trip east and close a deal with the gangsters. Then things get worse and worse—but at the end, they get better." A pretty routine formula for a film.

It was clear that Rock needed a fresh approach on the screen—and his next film was just what the doctor ordered . . . a comedic career transfusion!

★ 5 ★
THE *PILLOW TALK* YEARS
(1959–1965)

IN 1959, Rock Hudson's box-office popularity was at an all-time high. *Photoplay* magazine had awarded him the "Photoplay Gold Medal" as the favorite screen star of 1957 and 1958. The Theater Owners of America proclaimed him 1958's "Star of the Year." The following year, the Allied States Association of Motion Picture Exhibitors awarded him their "Star of the Year" certification, making him the first movie star to be heralded by both groups of national film exhibitors. However, his staying power required career growth.

After appearing in forty drama, melodrama, and adventure movies, it was time for a challenging change of pace. As had happened in 1954 with *Magnificent Obsession,* producer Ross Hunter was responsible for this particular metamorphosis.

"Me in a comedy?" an astounded Hudson asked Hunter when the idea of appearing in the witty contemporary comedy was first suggested. "I don't think I'm funny!" said Rock. Similarly, he argued with director Michael Gordon, "I've never been in comedy. I don't know how to play it." However, he was the first to admit, "By 1959 I was ready for a change. Any change. And I must say the studio came up with one."

Years later, Rock would look back and recall, "When they gave me the synopsis to read, I said I really couldn't do the film. It seemed to me dreadful. But then, a synopsis is not really a fair thing. It only gives you an inkling of what a story is about. You can tell whether you're supposed to be going down a jungle river or doing a love scene, and that's all a synopsis is good for. I mean, the shell of *Pillow Talk* is nothing. But when I read the script, I felt differently. The dialogue was really sharp."

Finally he consented and the whole experience was a sheer delight all the way around. Rock was to refer to the filming of *Pillow Talk* as "the most fun I'd ever had in front of a camera. The crew laughed. We laughed. It was almost a shame to take the paychecks!"

Originally entitled *Any Way the Wind Blows,* the sparkling comedy was to become a landmark in contemporary romantic comedy. It was retitled *Pillow Talk* before it was released.

Rock Hudson played Brad Allen, a successful songwriter who is simultaneously having affairs with several sexy girls, who are in awe of him. He shares a telephone "party line" with an independent career woman named Jan Morrow (Doris Day). Every time Jan tries to make a phone call, it seems that her phone line is always occupied by Brad Allen, who is usually serenading one of his female conquests.

Jan and Brad argue on the phone about each party listening in on the other's conversations. Jan pegs Brad as an oversexed wolf, and he infers that she is a frustrated and celibate matron.

It just so happens that Jan is being pursued by Jonathan Forbes (Tony Randall), who is Brad's close friend and business associate. Jonathan's description of Jan as a beautiful and bright girl persuades Brad to invent a fictitious identity and court Jan himself. Pretending to be an "aw shucks" Texas businessman named Rex Stetson, Brad sweeps Jan off her feet . . . until she finds out who he really is.

The situation is classic comedy, the dialogue is snappy and filled with innuendo, and Doris and Rock's performances redefined the American concept of contemporary career girls and swinging bachelors for many years to come. The supporting cast was also excellent, especially Thelma Ritter as Jan's dipsomaniacal housekeeper. The critics loved *Pillow Talk*.

Exclaimed *Variety*, "a sock box-office comedy. It is a sleekly sophisticated production that deals chiefly with s-e-x." *Redbook* compared it to *It Happened One Night* (1934), proclaiming it to be "brilliant," while the *Saturday Review* praised it for being "one occasion when everyone concerned seems to know exactly what he is doing."

Pillow Talk grossed $7.5 million and won an Academy Award for "Best Screenplay" (story and screenplay written directly for the screen). Doris Day received an Academy Award nomination for her portrayal of Jan Morrow.

Of one of the film's sequences, Rock Hudson was later to explain, "I have a confession to make about the long, climactic sequence in *Pillow Talk* where I sweep Doris out of bed and carry her through the lobby and down in the street. I hate to admit this, but Doris is a tall, well-built girl, and I just couldn't tote her around for as long and as far as required, so they built a special shelf for me with two hooks on it and she sat on the shelf, and all I did was hold her legs and shoulders. I could have managed if only one take had been involved, but we went on endlessly, primarily because there was a bit actor who played a cop on the street, and as we passed him,

Doris's line was 'Officer, arrest this man,' and the cop was supposed to say to me, 'How you doing, Brad?' But that stupid actor kept calling me Rock!" Sounds hauntingly similar to Rock's "bigger black-board" line from *Fighter Squadron!*

Said Hudson of the Rex Stetson character in *Pillow Talk*, "I had to use a phony Texas accent in this picture. For *Giant*, I had to acquire a true Texas dialect. But here, I had to hoke it up a little. I actually played to the crew—and broke them up. Before each scene, the director said: 'Be amused.' You can't just be amused. So before the camera started rolling, I'd say something in my Texan accent to get Doris laughing. The laughter began to mount. Doris and I broke up—laughing—and the cameras just kept rolling."

Doris sang the theme song for the movie, also entitled "Pillow Talk." During the film's action, Doris and Rock go out to a piano bar, where they join entertainer Perry Blackwell in a song called "Roly Poly." At the completion of the film, Doris's single version of "Pillow Talk" was released by Columbia Records. To add to the film's publicity, Rock also recorded his version of "Pillow Talk," backed with "Roly Poly" as a 45 rpm single for Decca. Said Hudson at the time, "I would like to make more records, and will, if this one sells." It didn't.

According to Rock he was never quite able to pin-point exactly what it was that made him appealing up on the screen. "I don't know what it is," he once commented. "I play my roles straight, and I do what I'm told. But people tend to identify an actor with the parts he plays. I've always had 'good guy' roles. I mostly get the girl. Maybe the fans think it'll get contagious, after a while."

One of the oddest things that happened to him occurred on a promotional tour. "When I was in

Chicago with *Pillow Talk*," he was later to recall, "in the late afternoon I had to go up to my hotel room, change my clothes, and get ready for a cocktail party. I walked in and began to peel. From the corner of my eye I saw something move. It was a woman asleep in a chair. Her daughter, four or five, was watching me round-eyed. The whole deal startled me, especially the little-girl part. The daughter said, 'Mommy, Mommy!' Mommy woke and said, 'I want to get into pictures. You're the only one who can help me.' I asked, 'But what can I do? I don't own any studios.' She said, 'I haven't any money. I am unhappy with my husband. I don't like Chicago and I want to go away.' I asked, 'Are those your only reasons for wanting to get into pictures? Don't you want to be an actress?' She said, 'Yes,' and I said, 'Why?' She said, 'All actresses are rich.' I said, 'I don't know whether you care what I think or not, but what I think is this: if you don't leave right now, I'm calling the manager.' I worried afterward about what I would have done if she'd started screaming and torn her clothes off. All hell would have popped."

In the fall of 1959, Rock was the celebrity host on a short-lived television show called *The Big Party*. The premise of the show was that each week a different star would host a party for several show-business friends. On hand for host Hudson's "Big Party" were Tallulah Bankhead, Esther Williams, Carlos Montoya, and Sammy Davis, Jr.

Rock's next film was *The Last Sunset* (1961), shot in Mexico during the summer of 1960. The outcome was a bit of a western soap opera, complete with incest and suspense. Rock plays lawman Dana Stribling, who is chasing the murderer of his brother-in-law. The outlaw is named Brendon O'Malley (Kirk Douglas), who runs into his ex-love, Belle Breckenridge (Dorothy Malone), since married to John

Breckenridge (Joseph Cotton). Brendon falls in love with Belle's daughter Missy (Carol Lynley), who turns out to be his daughter. A gunfight transpires between Dana and Brendon, leaving the outlaw dead and Dana and Belle free to ride off into the sunset. The film was a letdown after *Pillow Talk*.

The Last Sunset was the last film that Rock owed Universal-International on his existing contract. His new agreement with them was a "per picture" deal which left him free to take any additional film offers from other studios while being guaranteed two Universal films per year, at approximately $100,000 per film. His first film under this new agreement was the production of Seven Pictures, a producing company Hudson formed with his agent Henry Willson.

Hudson's first film under this new contractual arrangement was *Come September* (1961), which costarred Gina Lollobrigida, Sandra Dee, and Bobby Darin. Filmed in the fall of 1960 on location in Italy, Rock plays Robert Talbot, a rich American who makes a yearly trip each September to his villa on the Italian Riviera to visit his gorgeous mistress Lisa Filini (Lollobrigida). When he arrives unannounced one July, he discovers that his faithful right-hand-man (Walter Slezak) had been earning some extra cash by turning the villa into a hotel. The result was amusing, but not highly successful.

While in Rome in October 1960 working on the film, Rock reflected on his position in life, on his career, and on his ultimate ambitions. "I'm not satisfied all the time," he said. "I'm satisfied as far as work is concerned because I love it. What's not satisfying is when I try to go alone to take a walk. It's impossible then to have any peace of mind. I can't even go to movies anymore without being mobbed. It's true I always wanted to be a movie actor, hopefully a star. When I was a kid going to movies, I used to think how nice it would be to be in movies, and I used to read about the stars, but I never heard then of a lack of privacy."

As far as his ambitions, Rock pointed out that, "I'm happy as hell. But there are other things I want to do with my career. I don't know why, but I want to learn French and do a French picture with someone like Brigitte Bardot or Simone Signoret. I don't have a reason for wanting it—I just want it. I guess it's a difficult thing to do, so why not do it. Just like when I was a kid in Winnetka. Acting seemed like the hardest thing in the world for me. It was so unlikely, I was embarrassed to admit it to anyone.

"Anyway, besides doing a French movie, I'd like maybe in ten years to direct. And I'd like to branch out—to go on the stage because I think I have to try it. I think now maybe I can do other things. I remember I never used to go see myself in pictures because the sight of myself, the sound of my voice, used to make me cringe. Now I don't mind. I can tell when I do a good or bad scene, even though I can't always improve on it, because I know when the scenes were done, I did the best I could. But I think maybe there's been improvement. After all, I'm thirty-five years old now, I've been acting ten years, and I've lots more time to improve and to try other things. I'm not content. I still have ambition."

His next film was the much-demanded screen reunion with Doris Day. Happily, they took their magical movie chemistry to new heights with *Lover Come Back* (1961). The film has all of the appeal of *Pillow Talk*, with hilarious and well-timed comedy sequences throughout. Hudson and Day are competitive advertising agency executives, who become rivals for the same account.

Rock plays Jerry Webster, who convinces his boss, Peter Ramsey (Tony Randall), to allow him to produce a series of commercials for a nonexistent product called VIP. The ads were meant as a payoff for a showgirl named Rebel Davis (Edie Adams) who has given false testimony in Webster's favor before the Advertising Council. When his psychiatrist convinces him that he should be more assertive, neurotic Ramsey airs the seductive VIP ads.

When Carol Templeton (Doris Day) tries to steal the fictitious VIP account, she mistakes Webster for the scientist who has supposedly created VIP and attempts to persuade him that she should represent the product. In the meanwhile, Webster is trying to get her into bed. Pretending to be sexually inexperienced, Jerry Webster turns Carol into the aggressor. When she suddenly discovers his true identity, she explodes with anger. Finally, mad scientist Dr. Linus Taylor (Jack Kruschen) shows up with a product to match the name of VIP. It turns out to be candy wafers that the body converts into pure alcohol—equal to the potency of a triple martini. This is truly the best of the three Hudson/Day collaborations.

Not only did *Lover Come Back* match *Pillow Talk*'s box-office appeal, it exceeded it, grossing $8.5 million in America and Canada alone.

The Spiral Road (1962) was Rock's next screen outing. Here, as physician Dr. Anton Drager, he ventures to the jungle to learn all about leprosy from another medical man—Dr. Brits Jansen (Burl Ives). The picture was filmed on location in Dutch Guinea, with Gena Rowlands as Rock's leading lady.

A Gathering of Eagles (1963) found Hudson as airforce Colonel Jim Caldwell, a commander under the gun to perform his military duties at peak efficiency or end up "sacked" like his incompetent predecessor. Mary Peach plays his wife who finds adjusting to life at a Strategic Air Command base a bit hard to cope with. The supporting cast includes Kevin McCarthy and Rod Taylor. Taylor had last appeared with Rock in *Giant*, in which he played the husband of Hudson's sister-in-law.

His forty-seventh film was the on-screen and off-screen narrator of 20th Century–Fox's *Marilyn* (1963). The documentary tribute to Marilyn Monroe contained clips from fifteen of her films and, notably, footage from her final and uncompleted movie, *Something's Got to Give*.

In 1963, Rock Hudson's volume of fan letters reached 28,000 a week. That was the same year that he purchased a $180,000 Beverly Hills home for himself. He retained ownership of his Newport Beach house, which he turned over to his mother, Kay Olsen.

According to Kay, "If I tried to pick out my son's most outstanding characteristic, I'd have to say without hesitation that it is his wonderful ability to get a bang out of just about anything, anytime, anyplace. He might call me and say, 'Let's go to Las Vegas.' That doesn't mean next week or tomorrow. It means he is on his way over to pick me up. A lot of his friends think we are a little wacky, but you miss a lot of fun if you think up all the reasons why you shouldn't do this or that."

His friend Doris Day also agreed that Rock enjoyed his life to a great extent. They referred to each other as Doris Mary and Roy Harold, which were their original names before being "Hollywoodized." Said Doris, "Roy Harold is a dear, dear man. He gets such a kick out of little things, he laughs at silly things. He has the most wonderful laugh I've ever heard!

"I really do love him. He has all the qualities I like—simplicity, honesty, and most of all, a down-to-earth quality that most of us have when we're young but lose as we grow in our careers. Besides, he's an absolute nut!" Doris proclaimed.

Man's Favorite Sport? (1964) returned Rock to the comedy arena, but this time he is the brunt of the jokes in the script. The slapstick comedy was directed by Howard Hawks and costarred Paula Prentiss. Rock plays Roger Willoughby, who works at the famed sporting-goods store Abercrombie & Fitch in San Francisco and is the author of a guidebook on the subject of fishing. Unfortunately, he only knows about the theory of fishing—having never been on a fishing expedition himself.

Paula Prentiss is very funny as Abigail Page, a spunky press agent who comes up with the idea that it would be great publicity for the store to enter Roger in an upcoming fishing tournament. In the film, Rock plays straight man to Paula's gags. Sometimes they worked, sometimes they didn't.

When the film fizzled at the box office, Rock explained, "For me, in a comedy, the record tells us that I have to be the devil or the agitator, the one who plays the gag on someone else. I'm too big—apparently—to have the gag played on me, because the audience doesn't believe it or accept it. I played the buffoon. The joke was too strong; the revenge was too strong. I was uncomfortable playing it."

During production, Rock expressed his doubts about the film. "I fall into some mud, out of a tree, and off a motorcycle. A tent collapses on me and I get trapped in a sleeping bag. There's no script in this picture, just a story line. I'm used to having a script and building a character. I usually learn my lines at home at night before a scene, but I don't even get the lines on this picture until the day of filming. I've discovered that you really have to think and concentrate on each scene. It's really kind of ad lib. You can say anything you want, but the one thing you must have is a director who knows, one like Howard on this picture."

In retrospect, Rock was not so understanding of the director's techniques on this picture. Howard Hawks was responsible for several successful screen comedies in his career, most memorably the Katharine Hepburn/Cary Grant classic *Bringing Up Baby* (1938). On the subject of working with Hawks on *Man's Favorite Sport?* Rock admitted, "He'd made very many brilliant films. But it was like he'd given up. And therefore it was quite disillusioning. All of the jokes and comedic sequences in that film were repeats of things he'd done in his various other films. He would say that something was very funny in such and such a film he'd made before, and so we'd do it here. I think a director reaches a dangerous time in his life when he feels that anything he does is the best. Without trying. It's something that has happened to lots of them. Not to actors, though. I think actors always try. But some directors, after a while, don't try. No, not some—lots. Lots of very very successful, brilliant directors. It's heartbreaking to me when I see it happening, or see a film which is the result of it."

He further observed that "I've always played men of physical strength. In *Pillow Talk* I carried Doris Day for blocks. But in this picture I can't do anything. In my other films I was always the antagonist and in this I'm the victim."

In the early 1960s there had been talk of two film projects that never transpired. One was *Montezuma,* in which Rock was to play the title role to Kirk Douglas's portrayal of the conquistador Cortez. Also planned was *There Were These Two Irishmen,* in which

Rock Hudson as most people remember him—in the arms of Doris Day. Their three movies together made them the world's Number One screen couple in the late 1950s and early 1960s. Here they are on the set of their first box-office smash together, *Pillow Talk* (1959). *AP/Wide World Photos*

1954
Rock as *Taza, Son of Cochise.*

As Bick Benedict in *Giant.*
1957

AP/Wide World Photos

Sipping a cocktail in London.
1969

AP/Wide World Photos

1980
As Jason Rudd in *The Mirror Crack'd.*

1964
In *Man's Favorite Sport?*

Rock in *The Last Sunset.*
1961

AP/Wide World Photos

AP/Wide World Photos

1981 On TV's *The Devlin Connection.*

AP/Wide World Photos

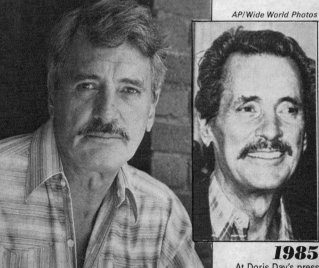

1985
At Doris Day's press conference.

AP/Wide World Photos

Rock chats with his costar Piper Laurie on the set of *The Golden Eagle* (1953). This adventure film was one of Hudson's first starring roles.
AP/Wide World Photos

With Elizabeth Taylor and Mercedes McCambridge on the set of the 1957 Texas epic *Giant,* for which Rock received his only Academy Award nomination.
AP/Wide World Photos

In 1963 Rock was awarded a Golden Globe as the "Male World Film Favorite" by the Hollywood Foreign Press Association. Jane Wyman, his love interest in *Magnificent Obsession* (1954) and *All That Heaven Allows* (1955), presents the trophy to Hudson.
AP/Wide World Photos

Rock relaxes between takes of the 1958 film *The Tarnished Angels* with his costar Dorothy Malone. *AP/Wide World Photos*

LEFT: Rock Hudson keeps Mae West warm as they rehearse their singing duet of "Baby, It's Cold Outside." Their performance was the most talked-about segment of the broadcast of the Academy Awards, March 26, 1958. Rock and Mae never completed the song, because they both started laughing so hard once they got into the number.
AP/Wide World Photos

Rock was the life of the party on October 12, 1959, when *Pillow Talk* premiered in New York City. Here he mesmerizes Gloria Swanson and Tallulah Bankhead at the gala celebration. *AP/Wide World Photos*

TOP: Rock poses with his mother Kay Olson and date Betty Abbott at the April 20, 1954, premiere of *Magnificent Obsession*. *AP/Wide World Photos*

MIDDLE: On November 9, 1955, Rock surprised everyone by eloping with Phyllis Gates. The marriage was to dissolve in 1959. *AP/Wide World Photos*

BOTTOM: Rock was in good company when four of Hollywood's leading men got together at Universal Studios on June 23, 1962. (Left to right: Rock Hudson, Cary Grant, Marlon Brando, and Gregory Peck.) *AP/Wide World Photos*

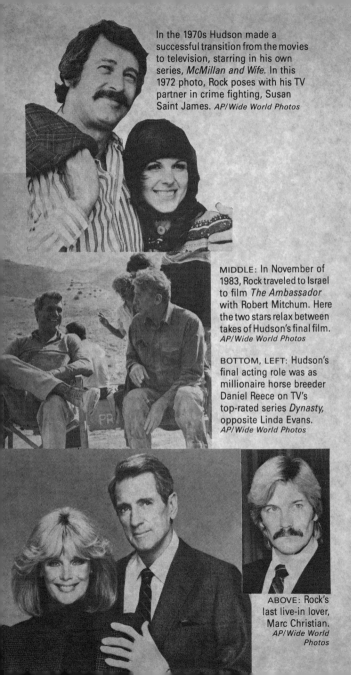

In the 1970s Hudson made a successful transition from the movies to television, starring in his own series, *McMillan and Wife*. In this 1972 photo, Rock poses with his TV partner in crime fighting, Susan Saint James. *AP/Wide World Photos*

MIDDLE: In November of 1983, Rock traveled to Israel to film *The Ambassador* with Robert Mitchum. Here the two stars relax between takes of Hudson's final film. *AP/Wide World Photos*

BOTTOM, LEFT: Hudson's final acting role was as millionaire horse breeder Daniel Reece on TV's top-rated series *Dynasty*, opposite Linda Evans. *AP/Wide World Photos*

ABOVE: Rock's last live-in lover, Marc Christian. *AP/Wide World Photos*

Rock Hudson, the seductively handsome screen idol, was a top movie star for four decades. This photo from 1957 shows off the clean-cut image that made him a star. *AP/Wide World Photos*

Rock would play a dual role as both a father and his son. Explained Rock of the latter project, "Six different writers tried it, but couldn't hack it, so we figured something had to be wrong with the basic story."

Hudson's next three films were to be comedies. *Send Me No Flowers* (1964) was the third and last of the Rock Hudson/Doris Day films. Said Doris at the time, "The first two were big hits. Maybe we're a lucky combination!" In this teaming the formula is altered slightly to find Hudson and Day as a man and wife living in suburbia. He is a hypochondriac who overhears his doctor talking about a patient who has two weeks to live and erroneously assumes that the physician is talking about him. Worried that he is going to leave his wife an unprovided-for widow, Rock enlists his best friend (Tony Randall) to help find a surrogate spouse for her and to assist him in picking out cemetery plots. The scene where Paul Lynde attempts to sell Rock gravesites is hysterical fun. Although a bit offbeat, *Send Me No Flowers* is an amusing collaboration by the hottest screen couple of the late 1950s and early 1960s: Doris Day and Rock Hudson.

Rock next filmed a rematch with Gina Lollobrigida in his fiftieth film, *Strange Bedfellows* (1964). She plays a pop art aficionado, and he is an oil tycoon. The comedy, which tends toward the slapstick variety, was filmed in London.

A Very Special Favor (1965) found Rock as close as he would come to doing that French picture that he spoke of starring in. His costars here are Leslie Caron and Charles Boyer. As Paul, Rock is asked by his lawyer friend (Boyer) to awaken the woman in his young daughter (Caron) by focusing his romantic charms on her. According to Hudson, "It's a sex picture, like the French and Italians make. I play an American millionaire, conscripted by Boyer to teach his serious, unmarried daughter, Leslie Caron, the facts of life. When I saw how far we were going with this sex business, I asked the director, Michael Gordon, to cut out those risqué scenes, but he didn't pay any attention to me. I was really perturbed about them."

He later criticized *A Very Special Favor* by explaining, "The things I had to do to Leslie Caron were cruel. They weren't funny for the sake of a joke. In her revenge, that was also too cruel; it completely castrated me and it didn't work. It was just too strong."

The December 20, 1963, issue of *Life* magazine contained a salute to "The Movies." Among the features in that issue was a photo spread entitled "Big Stars Take Old Roles." The spread was photographed by Bert Stern, and it featured Cary Grant as Charlie Chaplin, Audrey Hepburn as Pearl White (*The Perils of Pauline*), Tony Curtis as Rudolph Valentino in *The Son of the Sheik* (1926) with Natalie Wood as Vilma Banky, Paul Newman as swashbuckling Douglas Fairbanks, Sr., Frank Sinatra and Dean Martin as gladiators, Bing Crosby and Bob Hope as gangsters, Jack Lemmon as a World War I flying ace à la *Wings* (1927), Shirley MacLaine in a Busby Berkley fantasy, and last but not least, a two-page spread of Rock Hudson as Dr. Jekyll and Mr. Hyde (1920, 1932, and 1941).

Just like the two personalities housed in the body of Dr. Jekyll, there were two different sides of Rock Hudson's personal life during this era.

Publicly, during the early 1960s, Rock's most frequent date was singer Marilyn Maxwell. Gossip columnists were busy chasing down items about how he rushed to New York City to be at her side for her February 1962 club opening at the Latin Quarter, and about them supposedly shopping for wedding rings and spending Christmas of 1962 together in upstate New York. When one columnist quizzed Maxwell about the possibility of her becoming the second Mrs. Hudson, she replied, "Ask him—I'd like to know too."

"We're just friends," Rock informed the *New York Post*, but *Modern Screen* insisted, "As long as Rock keeps dating Marilyn Maxwell, you can be sure that their romance is still a living, growing relationship, and that they have not abandoned the idea of marriage."

On the other side of the fence, after Rock's death in 1985, several magazines reported that during this same era, Rock had met a young man who moved into his Beverly Hills home. Rock squired the former football player around Hollywood and introduced him to all the right people who could help the aspiring actor to get on his feet in show business. Several photographs of Rock Hudson and the young man exist, and several sources confirm his identity, so there is no question that the two men were friends.

However, when the unknown young actor got his first big break, landing a role on a national television series, he promptly moved out of Rock's house and acted as if he had never known Hudson for fear that it would ruin his macho image. Before Rock Hudson took him under his wing, no one in show business was acquainted with the ambitious young man. Yet as Rock's protégé, the young man ended up with his own agent and his start in show business. Since that time the "protégé" has starred in several national television series, and throughout his career, he has pretended that he never knew Rock.

Hudson's last twenty years in Hollywood included a succession of affairs with infamous, famous, and aspiring men. However, he was always quite discreet about his very active sex life. According to one noted agent, "Rock Hudson helped several people get started in show business."

★ 6 ★
THE ADVENTURE-FILM STAR (1966–1971)

EACH OF THE nine films that Rock Hudson starred in from 1966–1971 was of the adventure genre. Some were straight adventure, some were comical adventures, but all of them were very "action" based in their plots.

In the mid-1960s, spy and secret-agent films were all the rage. From James Bond on the big screen to *The Man From U.N.C.L.E.* on television, America couldn't seem to get enough of spys, counterspys, double agents, and all sorts of outlandish secret devices.

Blindfold (1966) found Rock playing the role of Dr. Bartholomew Snow, a prominent psychiatrist in Manhattan who is enlisted by the government to treat a key scientist (Alejandro Rey) who has suffered a total nervous breakdown. Hudson soon finds himself embroiled in an international plot. The scientist's sister, Victoria Vail (Claudia Cardinale), suspects Dr. Snow of being part of the plot to abduct her brother, who obviously knows more than he should. This film was actress Claudia Cardinale's first Hollywood movie. According to the show-biz weekly *Variety*, "Hudson offers one of his customary light portrayals, sometimes on the cloyingly coy side, and is in for more physical action than usual."

This film was the first product of Rock's new production company, aptly entitled Gibraltar Productions. Now Rock was in the driver's seat. "I got my wish," he explained before the cameras started rolling, "even if I had to form my own company to do it. Being my own boss gives me the opportunity to select my stories and pass judgment on cast and director. The first Gibraltar production is a suspense thriller, *Blindfold*, to be made in Florida and here [New York City], and to be released by Universal." His second Gibraltar-produced film was the thriller entitled *Seconds*.

Seconds (1966) offered a complete departure for Rock. Filmed in high-contrast black and white to accentuate the surreal nature of the plot, Hudson often commented that *Seconds* and *Giant* were two of his personal favorites among his sixty-five films.

The plot of *Seconds* deals with a highly mysterious organization that has the ability to give people a new lease on life . . . in fact it can give volunteers a totally new life. For the reasonable fee of thirty thousand dollars, a person can purchase a new face, new voice, new body, new profession, and a new identity. John Randolph plays Arthur Hamilton, a banker who is thoroughly bored with his existence. He pays the fee, undergoes surgery and complete therapy, and awakens feeling like a new person . . . literally! He is now Antiochus Wilson (Rock Hudson). What a bargain; certainly dozens of people would have gladly paid much more money to have become Rock Hudson in 1966!

Antiochus ends up taking off for Malibu, where he meets Nora Marcus (Salome Jens), who ends up being a "second" as well. He does new things, he meets new friends, then one night he gets smashed at a cocktail party and begins reminiscing about his old life as Arthur Hamilton. Poor choice of cocktail-party subjects, especially when there are other "seconds" at the party who don't want their covers blown. Antiochus is shipped back to the organization, where he asks to be transformed back to his former self. Instead, the organization transforms Antiochus into a corpse.

When the film was screened at the Cannes Film Festival, the critics hated it so much that the film's director, John Frankenheimer, refused to attend the planned press conference, and Rock went instead, to listen to the reporters blast the film as totally inhumane. The critic for the *Saturday Review*, however, glowed. "I haven't seen a better American film all this year . . . Hudson is just about perfect as a 'reborn.' "

According to Rock Hudson, "What I liked was the fact that the story wasn't really told until after the film had been seen. Or, in my own case, until after I had finished reading the script before I made the film. For some strange reason it's only truly told when you think back on it. I mean, that clinic is a death clinic. But as you watch the movie you don't feel that. You're thinking of these unfortunate people who can't grapple with life the way they are, so they change for a better life—for nothing. Meanwhile the clinic has gotten rich from the assets of the clients. Just flat rich. That's what made it terrifying for me. And equally, that's what made it intriguing to do."

In 1966, Rock Hudson was Carol Burnett's guest star on her weekly comedy/variety television series. One of the skits that Rock performed with Carol was a mock western in which Hudson made his TV singing and dancing debut. He had danced the Charleston in *Has Anybody Seen My Gal?* in 1952, and he had sung a couple of times on camera in *Pillow Talk* in 1959, but he had never done either in front of a live audience. When Hudson recalled this skit on the Burnett show, he said, "The cameras were rolling and the director gave me my cue. I froze. I was disgraced. The director hollered for the crew to hold the tape and start over again. The audience broke up!" It wasn't until a number of years later . . . with Carol Burnett by his side, that Rock was able to make his actual musical-comedy theatrical debut.

When Rock Hudson filmed *Tobruk* (1966), it represented his last film under contract to Universal. From *Undertow* in 1949 to *Tobruk* in 1966, his working relationship with Universal-International had produced forty-five of his fifty-four films to date (in 1973 he was to star in *Showdown* for Universal, as an independent player).

In the mid seventies Hudson spoke about choosing the right scripts. "Usually I can smell a failure as soon as I read the script," he proclaimed. "I can't smell a hit, though. If I could do that, I'd be a multimillionaire. But I cannot. Nobody can. Mainly I have been under contract to a studio where I was governed. But I still had my own thoughts, you see. I mean, I would go into a film if the studio said I had to. And sometimes I would either think or say that it was a bunch of crap. I'd say, 'Watch and see. It won't make any money.' But, nevertheless I made it. I was obligated. Did you ever start to read a book and never finish it? Well, it's like that with me if I'm stuck with a poor script. It just feels as if there's no point in continuing on. I could name you many examples from the movies I've made. The most recent would be *Tobruk* or *Showdown*."

Tobruk features Hudson as Major Donald Craig and George Peppard as Captain Kurt Bergman, two Allied soldiers out to outsmart the Nazis in World

War II by blowing up the enemy's supply of gasoline in the Sahara Desert. Rock is rescued by German-born Palestinian Jews, who assist him in his mission. The exploding gasoline provides the most colorful moment of the film.

On September 29, 1967, Rock Hudson was one of the stars of a television special called "The Hollywood Musicals," which was part of the *Kraft Music Hall* series. His costars were Connie Stevens, Michelle Lee, and Bobby Van. Encouraged by his performance on Carol Burnett's show the previous season, Hudson even tried his hand at some singing and dancing. "They've kept the dance steps fairly simple and they kind of lead me through them, but I get the hang of it pretty well," he said. "For instance, I play the stage manager in a segment satirizing the business about the understudy who gets her big break opening night when the leading lady breaks her leg. And I sing!"

Since his Universal contract had expired as of June 1966, it was a time of career reflection for Rock. "Financially, it hasn't been a good year," he admitted, "but I had to make a decision, expensive as it was, to do nothing. The last four or five films I made were mediocre. I was not improving as an actor. I needed time to reevaluate myself. I needed to figure out, 'What's wrong? What's good, or is it good? Do I want this, or am I going through the motions?' " His next film choice, however, was a winner.

In *Ice Station Zebra* (1968) Rock Hudson stars as Commander James Ferraday, who is in charge of a nuclear submarine headed for the North Pole. His mission is to get up to an encampment known as Ice Station Zebra—immediately—before the Russians can beat him there. An airlift is impossible as there is an ice storm in progress that may take weeks to subside.

Ferraday is in the dark about the ultimate mission, and the specific task is to be performed by a British intelligence agent, Brian Jones (Patrick McGoohan). During their submarine journey, two more personnel are airlifted aboard the submarine: Boris Vaslov (Ernest Borgnine), a defected Russian agent, and an American named Captain Leslie Anders (Jim Brown). Ferraday is a bit suspicious of Jones, Valsov, and Anders. Something is up and he can't figure out exactly what it is.

As Ferraday, Rock's acting job consists mainly of pacing the submarine's floor space, knitting his brows, and looking distrustingly at all three key members of the top-secret mission. When the submarine arrives at the North Pole, it is revealed exactly who in the cast is not whom he is pretending to be. *Ice Station Zebra* features some great special-effects photography, especially when the submarine goes under the northern icecap. When the submarine unsuccessfully tries to break through the ice on its first attempt, the whole sub is shaken. Always retaining his cool, Rock simply gets on the intercom and announces, "This is the captain! Sorry about that."

During another attempt, severe damage occurs, apparently by sabotage, and the results are almost fatal. Surviving narrowly, Hudson again takes hold of the microphone and announces, "We're on our way up. Everything is under control." That was the Rock Hudson that the world fell in love with—the hero who is always "under control."

Based on the novel by espionage pro Alistair MacLean, *Ice Station Zebra* was one of the high points of Rock's adventure-film phase. The screen version of this story features plenty of well-executed action scenes, plenty of plot twists, and a sweeping musical score by Michel Legrand. With its all-star, all-male cast, *Ice Station Zebra* is also known as Howard

Hughes's favorite film. He was known to watch it over and over again in his private screening room!

This film was to be Rock Hudson's last big money-making movie, earning $4.8 million in theatrical release in the United States and Canada. Although he was to make ten more movies, this was to be his last big cinema career peak. The film included several scenes actually shot in the Arctic North, but most of the action was lensed at the M-G-M back lot in Hollywood, during some of 1968's hottest weather.

A Fine Pair (1969) reteamed Rock with Italian beauty Claudia Cardinale. This Italian-produced comedy stars Hudson as New York City police Captain Mike Harmon, who is tricked into assisting jewel thief Esmeralda Marini (Cardinale), with whom he has fallen in love. An amusing idea, the film did not work, neither on screen nor at the box office.

Rock's next release was *The Undefeated* (1969), in which he costarred with John Wayne. The action begins right at the end of the Civil War. As Confederate Colonel James Langdon, Hudson sets fire to his plantation rather than let the Northern carpetbaggers get hold of his possessions, and he heads for Mexico. He has been promised that he will be met by representatives of Emperor Maximilian's army. In the meanwhile, former Union Colonel John Henry Thomas (John Wayne) is heading for Mexico as well, where he intends to sell three thousand horses to Maximilian's army for a neat little profit.

Although Langdon still holds a grudge against the "Yankees," he is constantly finding himself in dangerous situations that Thomas and his men are perpetually bailing him out of. When the Confederates are duped into becoming pawns for Benito Juárez's army, Thomas again comes to the rescue. Also in the cast are football players-turned-actors Merlin Olsen and Roman Gabriel. Said Hudson of his only film with John Wayne, "It was a pleasant experience. Duke was a wonderful person and a pleasure to work with."

When Blake Edwards made the satirical film *S.O.B.* (1981) about trying to save a musical film that is disastrously in production, the film that he was making fun of was his own box-office turkey, *Darling Lili* (1970). Starring Rock Hudson and Julie Andrews, *Darling Lili* is a musical spy spoof à la Mata Hari. Julie plays British music-hall entertainer Lili Smith, who is trying to pry war secrets out of flying ace Major William Larrabee (Rock). Lili is actually a German spy, but she naturally falls in love with Larrabee.

Rock agreed that the resulting film was one big mess, and he and Blake Edwards ended up hating each other by the time the filming was completed. Recalls one inside source, "Something happened, and Blake Edwards went after him in a mean way. There were all sorts of items in the gossip columns about what was going on, on the set."

Hudson's opinion of *Darling Lili* was that, "It should have been played as 'high camp,' what with such great lines as, 'I fly at dawn!' " The movie premiered, and closed, at movie theaters in rapid succession.

Rock, whose last two movies were released in the opposite order from which they were filmed, commented that he was happily keeping busy as he entered his third decade as a star. Said Hudson, "We were eight months chasing through Europe before returning to Hollywood to finish *Darling Lili* with Julie Andrews. And after that Duke Wayne and I were all over the South and in Durango, Mexico, on long locations, making *The Undefeated*. I'm not downgrading all those comedies with Doris [Day]—they were keeping with the mood of the audiences then and they certainly kept me in fine style. But I'm glad

I've been able to move on to completely different things. It's not easy convincing producers to forget a former image."

Next on the movie agenda was *Hornet's Nest* (1970). As Captain Turner, Rock finds himself in World War II again; this time around he is on a sabotage mission, aided by a gang of Italian orphans and a beautiful female doctor named Bianca (Sylva Koscina). Explained Hudson, "What do I think of dirty pictures? Well, I better think pretty well of at least one of them—*The Hornet's Nest*, which I made in Italy. In it, I use four-letter words, beat up and rape my costar, Sylva Koscina, and generally behave like any good World War II soldier shouldn't. I'll say this for the picture, sensationalism isn't just dragged in for the purpose of competing with the flood of stag movies being released in the art houses. Given the set of circumstances he has to cope with, the man I play is not out of character. And that's no cop-out."

In September 1969, Rock Hudson volunteered to embark on a seventeen-day "handshake tour" of combat bases in Vietnam. He departed from Italy, where he was working on *Hornet's Nest*, and flew to Vietnam. The jaunt was organized through the Hollywood Overseas Committee and the USO.

Always one to try something new, in 1970 Rock Hudson recorded an album entitled *Rock, Gently* (Stanyon Records, 1970). It was produced by Rod McKuen, a friend from his days on the Universal-International lot. Rod had long since given up on his movie career and had become quite successful as a best-selling poet who recorded his recitation/songs to music. The biggest hit he had written was "Jean" (the theme from *The Prime of Miss Jean Brodie*).

The fourteen songs on *Rock, Gently* were all written by McKuen and are lushly orchestrated. All of the selections are ballads, and Rock does all of his own singing without any sort of vocal background.

"Terrifying!" is how Hudson found his first recording session since 1959's "Pillow Talk"/"Roly Poly" single release. "It was such a shock to hear myself on playback," he explained. "I don't mean hearing the voice, because I had heard that a dozen times, but what I thought was right was so totally wrong. Being an actor is a visual medium and making a record is only vocal. So you must try to put over every form of emotion through the voice and not through the eyes. I didn't know that.

"We tried it seven or eight times and when it still wouldn't work, I tried another song. On that first recording session I worked from ten in the morning until eleven that night. At the end of the first day I was loose enough to say, 'That was a mistake, now I know how to do it.' It took three days to loosen up properly. It took two weeks to do all the songs. We were supposed to do enough for one album, but we ended up with enough for three," said Rock, who recorded the LP in London in March 1970.

The record is, in a word, dreadful. The songs are all so maudlin and depressing that Hudson sounds like a hound howling at the moon. If he had attempted some bawdy drinking songs like the one he sang in *All That Heaven Allows* in 1955, he might have pulled it off. But listening to this record is torture, especially rock's rendition of "Jean." He should, however, be saluted for trying this project—even if the best thing about it is the album cover!

His next film, *Pretty Maids All in a Row* (1971), was a complete change of pace for Hudson, as this time around he played the villain. Director Roger Vadim's first American feature film, *Pretty Maids* was produced by Gene Roddenberry of "Star Trek" fame. As Michael "Tiger" McDrew, Rock plays a high-school football coach and guidance counselor who goes berserk. He seduces and then murders several of the pretty girls attending the high school where he works. Also in the cast are Angie Dickinson, Telly Savalas, and Roddy McDowall.

According to Hudson, "I had read the book on which the film is based and thought, 'How could they get a screenplay out of this trash?' But then they sent me the script, and I enjoyed the brazenness of the character. He is a kind of mastermind, manipulating everyone. To me, he's a very intriguing character. A part of a totally insane world. A real schizo behind a Mr. Nice Guy facade.

"Vadim has what every great director must, and that is the presence to make actors on the set want to work harder," said Rock. In one scene Rock appears to be nude, but the scene was actually an illusion, as the shot was done from the waist up. Said Hudson on the subject, "Nudity is fine in a film when it is used within the context of the story. It becomes offensive when it is exploited. The same goes for swearing in a film."

In 1959, when Rock starred in the debut episode of the television series *The Big Party*, he was quoted as saying, "I've wanted to get into television for a long while, but my picture contract prohibited it." After holding out on television for so long, in the 1970s he was about to embark on a whole new phase of his career. It was to represent a fresh new audience for his acting talents, and he was to become known as one of the most successful television actors who had made the transition from movie star to TV star, only adding to his already well-established appeal.

★ 7 ★
BIG SCREEN/LITTLE SCREEN
(1971–1985)

HAVING ACTED in sixty different movies, by 1971, the idea of starring in a 104-minute feature film that just happened to be produced by a television network (NBC) hardly seemed like much of a departure for Rock when he signed to do *Once Upon a Dead Man*. In it he was to play San Francisco Police Commissioner Stewart McMillan, with Susan Saint James as his bantering wife, Peggy McMillan. Broadcast on September 17, 1971, *Once Upon a Dead Man* dealt with a criminal case involving a stolen sarcophagus, and naturally Hudson and Saint James are called in to solve the mystery of the robbery. The chemistry between Rock and Susan was very appealing, and the script was full of the same comedy elements that made the William Powell/Myrna Loy *Thin Man* series of films of the 1930s such a smash.

The ratings of *Once Upon a Dead Man* were impressive enough for NBC to offer Hudson a regular gig as Police Commissioner McMillan. Rock wasn't interested in doing a regular weekly series, but the deal that NBC was offering encompassed only one episode a month. Called *McMillan and Wife*, the show would alternate with two other detective series that were in production, *Columbo* (starring Peter Falk) and *McCloud* (starring Dennis Weaver). It was the perfect setup; Rock enjoyed working with Susan Saint James, and the scripts were consistently entertaining. The show was originally broadcast on Wednesday nights but was switched to Sundays. Among the cast highlights was the addition of a wisecracking maid played by Nancy Walker.

According to Hudson, "It's a unique idea—combining mystery and comedy. I really think it's the format. I am only on once a month. I didn't want to be on once a week. In TV, you have to make quick decisions, and you had better make the right decisions. TV is tougher than the 'B' pictures I did. What we're doing is making an hour-and-a-half movie every third week, playing the same characters like Bill Powell and Myrna Loy did in a number of *Thin Man* movies. I'd go nuts in a regular series, playing the same damn thing over and over."

Another nice aspect of *McMillan and Wife* was the fact that Rock Hudson was such an established celebrity draw that he was paid fifty thousand dollars per episode. The consistent income was perfect, since he was not contracted to receive a regular salary from a film studio, as he had been for all of his years at Universal. The series ran until 1975, when Susan Saint James and Nancy Walker left the show. The show's format was changed and retitled *McMillan*. Martha Raye was brought in as the sister of Nancy Walker's maid character, and Jessica Walter was contracted to portray Commissioner McMillan's new love interest. Oddly enough, both *McMillan and Wife* and *McMillan* were produced by Universal.

Since the series only occupied several months a year and then went into reruns in the spring, Rock found time to pursue other projects. In 1973 he starred with Dean Martin in the movie *Showdown*, which was his sixty-first (not-made-for-TV) movie. The turn-of-the-century western was about two old friends who are in love with the same woman (Susan Clark), with Rock as Sheriff Chuck Jarvis and Dean as his former-pal-turned-outlaw. While on location in New Mexico, Rock had an automobile accident that put him in the hospital for ten weeks with a couple of broken bones.

According to Hudson, "I considered myself very lucky—I could have been killed. I broke a leg, elbow, both wrists, and three ribs. I also had a concussion. Outside of that"—he laughed— "everything was just fine. I was on location in New Mexico, learning how to drive a 1904 Locomobile for my role. I was practicing by myself one Sunday on a real miserable washboard road when I lost control of the car. It careened into a tree and flipped over—and I flew through the air and slammed into a cement wall. My head was bleeding and I was slipping in and out of consciousness while the ambulance rushed me to the hospital. A doctor there, probably a 'fill-in,' because it was Sunday, examined me. 'You seem to be okay,' he said. It's hard to believe that all happened to me!"

In July 1973, upon the coaxing and support of his dear friend Carol Burnett, Rock made his musical-theater debut at L.A.'s Huntington Hartford Theater, in a production of the Broadway hit *I Do! I Do!* Said Rock, "We had to try out in San Bernardino [California]. That was my first time on the stage. When the curtain goes up, we are seated on the stage, and I have the opening lyrics. Because the stage was small, they had to push the curtain to let me sit down. So I actually FELT the curtain go up! My heart jumped into my throat and I knew I was not going to be able to sing. Happily the audience burst into applause. It lasted a minute or so and it gave me time to push my heart back where it belongs. From then on everything was easy. I could not wait to go to the theater and do it all over again."

The play was staged by Gower Champion and was so successful that the following summer Hudson and Burnett took the show on the road and broke attendance records when they played St. Louis, Washington, D.C., and Dallas, Texas. Rock was never much of a singer, but as Burnett proudly pointed out, "Of course, people would knock down doors just to watch him breathe."

According to Hudson at the time, "It is so much fun! Carol and I are having such a good time doing it that it would have been worth it even if I had fallen on my face."

In February 1976, Rock reprised his stage role when he and Juliet Prowse took a new production of *I Do! I Do!* to London. The critics were not too kind to Hudson, but the audiences loved it, and the limited eight-week run was sold out before the play even opened. According to the *London Sun*, Juliet Prowse "is fast enough on her feet to prevent any damage to her toes when Rock is called on to do an occasional, stiff-backed, military two-step."

When he returned to the United States, Hudson immediately signed to do a twenty-week American tour with Claire Trevor, Leif Erickson, and the Voices of Young America. Performing the dramatic narrative poem *John Brown's Body*, Rock was becoming quite at home performing before live audiences.

According to Rock, the theater work afforded him a nice break from his regular *McMillan* stint. "Five years is enough of any characterization—or it is for me. Not that I haven't enjoyed the series, even been proud of some of the segments. But if I hadn't had time off for *I Do! I Do!*, that wonderful stage fling with Carol, and some TV guest shots in other shows—well, I could have gone bananas playing one role for four years. I'm a movie star at heart."

Expressing a bit of frustration over the *McMillan*

character's stagnation, Rock voiced his opinion that "For a time I wanted to shake McMillan out of his post as police commissioner, have him resign, and go detective or private eye. It would have loosened him up—given us more leeway in the character. But NBC said a loud 'No!' The idea was, 'Don't muck up something going well.' "

Being just "a movie star at heart," in 1976 Rock signed to make his first foray into the science-fiction genre. In *Embryo*, a variation on the theme of the "test tube baby," Hudson plays a scientist named Dr. Paul Holliston who discovers the chemical process for taking a fetus, accelerating its growth, and raising it in a matter of days to maturity. Like Pavlov, he begins with dogs and graduates to experimenting with humans.

Dr. Holliston has a chip on his shoulder. His wife died and he always wanted another child. He has a grown son and a pregnant daughter-in-law, but takes the single-parent task to a new extreme. Using an aborted fetus from a local hospital, he turns his laboratory experiment into fully grown Barbara Carrera. What he doesn't realize is that the end product has a serious flaw. Victoria (Carrera) is addicted to a hormone known as "placental lactogen," derived from pregnant women, who must die for her to live. Hudson starts out as a Dr. Frankenstein in love with his monster, he graduates to Henry Higgins as he shapes her knowledge, and eventually he wants to bed down with his creation. This gives way to Rock's first totally nude scene in a movie. Dr. Holliston realizes that the experiment has gotten out of hand when Victoria eyes his daughter-in-law and her fetus as a dinner entrée!

According to Rock, "Something else that appealed to me about *Embryo* was that I couldn't put a classification on it. I mean, I wouldn't call it science fiction, because to me that denotes something like *Journey to the Center of the Earth* or *20,000 Leagues Under the Sea*. I see the story of *Embryo* primarily as a tragedy— the tragedy of a man who dedicated his life to what he felt was a good thing, as opposed to an evil thing . . . and who was not successful."

In the early 1970s the rumors of Rock Hudson's homosexuality again surfaced. This time they stemmed from a practical joke that a gay couple dreamed up in San Francisco. Known for their outrageous parties, the couple sent out party invitations to many of their friends announcing a reception for the wedding of Rock Hudson and Jim Nabors. When members of the press got hold of the mock wedding invitation, the repercussions opened up an old wound. Hudson, with his long-established macho image, was able to shrug off the joke as a vicious rumor. Nabors, however, who was signed to CBS-TV in 1971 for his own variety show, immediately found his series canceled. If it weren't for Hollywood friends like Burt Reynolds, who cast Nabors in his movies, Jim might never have appeared on camera again. He immediately left Hollywood and moved to Hawaii.

San Francisco writer and Hudson confidant, Armistead Maupin, said after Hudson's death, "Rock used to explain the story at dinner parties. In point of fact, he and Nabors were just good friends. But the rumor made it impossible for them to be seen together, which is very sad." Rock's stock answer, when the matter was repeatedly brought up by the press, was always "no comment."

This whole fictitious "wedding" episode caused Hudson to become quite leery of the press. "I enjoy playing the game with the press," he was later to explain. "It's fun to see how my answers are interpreted and how my personality and character are portrayed. I like to keep my secrets to myself and I guess they will die with me. I like to keep the journalists puzzled. The charm is in the guessing."

His avoidance of interviews gave him the reputation for being a horrible interview. "I'm terrible," he admitted in early 1985. "I was interviewed up the ass and I really had nothing to say. I didn't want to say anything because I knew it would be in print, so I got uptight. That's where I got that reputation. If there was a bad story, it used to hurt. It doesn't hurt anymore."

It was known by many of his close friends that in the late 1970s and early 1980s, Rock was living with a male companion named Tom Clark. Since Hudson had fired his agent/manager Henry Willson in the early 1960s, in interviews Clark was simply referred to as Rock's "manager."

During the early 1970s, Tom Clark worked as a publicist for M-G-M. It was there that he met Rock and eventually went to work for him as a money manager, secretary, and confidant. Rock was known by his friends as a man who loved to have a good time, and he could really "put away" a lot of liquor, especially Scotch. Tom was always there for Rock when the two of them went out drinking or "bar hopping." In fact he did everything for Rock.

One close friend of Rock's explained, "It came to the point that he was so dependent on Tom, because Tom babied him: he made sure Rock had a warm sweater on, he made his plane reservations, he made his dinner reservations, he made sure that Rock's clothes were out of the dry cleaners, he did everything for him. Rock loved that."

When Rock came to New York City, he liked to go down to the gay bars in Greenwich Village. One friend of his remembers, "If Rock wanted to go to a bar to 'cruise,' Tom would at least get him there, but he would never stay with him. Those were the only times that he would leave Rock alone, when he'd come down to the Ninth Circle. Rock used to love downstairs at the Ninth Circle where all the boys are. Tom would leave him there. Those were the only times that Tom would say, 'You're on your own.' "

In 1977, at the age of seventy-seven, Rock Hudson's mother, Kay Wood Shearer Fitzgerald Olsen died. She had lived all of these years in the Newport Beach house that her son had given her in 1963. Said Rock, "I made sure she had a good life as well as I could give for her, [I] sent her on trips—she loved to travel. [I] sent her around the world twice."

Hudson's next film was *Avalanche* (1978), which was produced by Roger Corman. Costarring Mia Farrow, *Avalanche* was a "disaster film" on two different counts: its format, and its critical and box-office reception. The 1970s had already seen a new wave of large-cast special-effects movies including *Earthquake* (1974), *Towering Inferno* (1974), and *Hurricane* (made-for-TV 1974), so *Avalanche* was a new twist on the formula of man vs. earth, wind, and fire. Both Hudson and Farrow appear to be bored out of their minds, and in adding the only excitement in the film, the snowstorm emerges as the hero rather than the villain. Buried in mountains of artificial snow, the actors look more like they've attended the ultimate Hollywood cocaine party instead of an avalanche.

"It's about a ski resort and how an avalanche destroys a town once trees have been removed to make ski runs," explained Rock, who was later to admit, "It was an 'el cheapo.' I thought no one would see it. I was not selective enough." His reason for the film was strictly financial, or as he put it "because I needed some dough."

Avalanche was filmed at Tamarron, a ski resort near Durango, Colorado. In the film, Rock plays the greedy owner of a ski lodge who is only interested in getting rich quick. One hopes his character, David Shelby, carried a good insurance policy. The acting in the film was decidedly "grade Z."

Also in 1978, Rock starred in his first television mini-series, *Wheels*, based on the Arthur Hailey novel of the same name. In the Detroit-based soap opera, Hudson played Adam Trenton, the head of an automotive company. Rock explained, "I was advised not to read the book, there were so many changes in it, so I didn't." He said of the car he introduces in the series, "The Hawk, you may know, was based on Ford's introduction of the Mustang, which saved the company." The five-part, ten-hour series did very well in the ratings and was later trimmed down to a shorter version.

One of the things that he was required to do in the filming of *Wheels* that was new to him was hitting his leading lady. His target was Lee Remick, who played his wife Erica Trenton. Said Rock, "Hitting an actress was a first for me. We rehearsed the scene carefully. But when the cameras were rolling, my hand seemed paralyzed. I couldn't force myself to hit Lee. It was as if some invisible force held back my hand."

In the late 1970s, Rock toured with two more theatrical musicals, *Camelot* and *On the Twentieth Century*. He was reportedly very excited about his role in the 1977 production of *Camelot*, and he was very much looking forward to bringing the production into New York City's Lincoln Center. However, composer/playwright Alan J. Lerner didn't want Rock's version competing with his plans to bring another production to Broadway. Said Hudson, "He's bringing the show into Manhattan next year with its original cast, and he was afraid I'd water down the impact of his production [starring Richard Harris]."

According to Rock he had always wanted to appear on Broadway, and he thought that the idea of playing Lincoln Center would be great for the critics to get used to him as a stage commodity. He explained that the Lincoln Center idea "was the one thing that sparked my interest in the tour. I know I would have been the target of the New York critics—and that I'd have to be perfect in the show. Without that goal, I simply lost interest in *Camelot.*"

His next theatrical venture was the 1979 touring company of the Broadway hit *On the Twentieth Century*, which took him to Chicago and Detroit, among other American cities. According to the *Chicago Sun-Times*, Rock was less than perfect: "His acting here is simply going through strenuous motions, and his singing, when it has to subside to less than a roar, is painfully off-key."

"When I was on tour with *On the Twentieth Century*," said Hudson, "I switched on the television in my Chicago hotel room and they were showing *Giant*. Usually I don't watch my old films on the tube, but this time I did. Particularly the middle bit, where they aged me. I wanted to see what I looked like. Well, it was extraordinary. When I went to the mirror to compare, I looked exactly the same. Yet I was just twenty-nine when I made that film. Recently, people have come up with a couple of ideas for sequels. One was straight follow-up, with Elizabeth [Taylor] and myself [*Giant II*]. The other was a TV series. I had a couple meetings about the film but decided I wasn't interested. I told the producers, 'If you do this, you would have to improve on the original. How can you improve on *Giant?*' I meant it, too. Forgetting that I was in it, I still think it was a perfect movie."

In 1980, Ross Hunter was talking about mounting a *Pillow Talk II* production for Rock Hudson and

Doris Day. "The script is being written right now and Rock has agreed. In fact, he can't wait. As soon as Doris gives her okay, we'll start filming. But if she decides she doesn't want to do the picture, we'll find another actress. She seems very interested and I think she really wants to do the picture," claimed Hunter. The new version would find Rock and Doris married and parents of a teenage daughter (Kristie McNichol); Gregory Harrison of TV's "Trapper John" would provide her love interest and Maureen Stapleton would take the Thelma Ritter role. This production fantasy of Ross Hunter's, however, never got off the ground.

What did happen, happily, was the screen reunion of Rock Hudson and Elizabeth Taylor in *The Mirror Crack'd* (1980). Based on the Agatha Christie murder mystery of the same name, the film was a witty and sparkling whodunit that found Hudson in an all-star cast including Angela Lansbury, Kim Novak, Geraldine Chaplin, and his friend since their Universal-International days together: Tony Curtis.

Rock and Liz hadn't been on the screen together since *Giant* in 1956, and their scenes together provide some of the film's most amusing moments. Hudson hadn't been in a film with Tony Curtis since they both had bit parts in *Winchester '73* and *I Was a Shoplifter*, both from 1950.

The bitchy Elizabeth Taylor/ Kim Novak dialogues in this film are hysterical, and obviously were mirrored in *Dynasty*'s Alexis/Krystle catfights on television. Angela Lansbury was so good as Agatha Christie's sleuth Miss Marple that she ended up with her own television show inspired by this portrayal (*Murder She Wrote*). This film isn't in the *Gone with the Wind* league ... unless it's compared to *Avalanche*. However, it is totally entertaining, classy, funny, and a fitting film to remember the Rock Hudson of the

1980s by. This was the last Hudson film released in theaters, and from this point on he began to have health problems.

The plot of *The Mirror Crack'd* concerns a movie star named Marina Gregg (Taylor) who is returning to the screen after a mysterious nervous breakdown. Her husband is the film's director, Jason Rudd (Hudson), her catty costar is voluptuous Lola Brewster (Novak), and the producer is Marty N. Fenn (Curtis). At a fete for the Hollywood notables, a young woman is poisoned, and it looks like someone is out to kill Marina Gregg.

At one point in the film, Rock gets to explain the movie business to the local vicar: "The producer supplies all the money, the director spends it . . . the director gets all the credit, the producer gets an ulcer."

Many of the film's campier moments are jibes at previous Rock Hudson movies. When a heavier than usual Liz runs across her bedroom and throws herself on top of Rock, who is lying on his back on the bed, movie audiences literally howled with laughter at this reunion of the *Giant* costars, for fear Hudson had been crushed by a plump Taylor. In another segment, Liz gazes into the mirror of her vanity table and ponders on her reflection while reciting, "Bags, bags, go away; Come right back on Doris Day!" The camera immediately cuts to the reaction on Rock's face, which is a look of shock at this "dig" at his *Pillow Talk* costar.

Contrasting with the look that Rock would have in 1984 and 1985, here we see that Hudson had developed quite an extended gut. His initial *Dynasty* episodes, compared to these scenes in *The Mirror Crack'd*, are evidence of his extreme weight loss in a short time span.

His familiarity to television audiences led to additional work in the 1980s in TV mini-series and in made-for-television movies. *The Martian Chronicles* (1980) was Hudson's second science-fiction venture, yielding an entertaining three-part, six-hour telecast based on Ray Bradbury's best-selling novel of the same name. Compared to *Star Wars*, some of the special effects are decidedly cheap, but the essence of the book is nicely retained. As Colonel John Wilder, Rock's character ultimately unlocks the mystery of the Martian civilization. He is the "constant" character of all three episodes, which chronicles the first attempts at the exploration of Mars, the inadvertent destruction of the Martian race, the Earthlings' colonization of the red planet, man's senseless nuclear destruction of Earth, and Hudson's realization that he and his family (wife and two children) are among the last human beings in existence.

The Martian Chronicles is divided into three distinct chapters: "Volume 1: The Expeditions," "Volume 2: The Settlers," and "Volume 3: The Martians" (available on video). The entire Martian race is destroyed via an infectious germ that man brings from Earth. Ironically, in less than five years Earth would in reality be faced with a new germ that would threaten it, and ultimately destroy Rock Hudson: AIDS.

In 1981 Rock starred in the NBC mini-series *The Starmaker*, costarring Suzanne Pleshette, Melanie Griffith, Brenda Vaccaro, and Ed McMahon. The plot concerned a Hollywood film director and his notorious casting couch. One of Hudson's character's "discoveries" was played by Kristian Alfonso, who now is in the TV soap opera *Days of Our Lives*. Recalls Alfonso, "I was very nervous about playing opposite Rock because he was such a big star. He was very gracious and fatherly to me. He calmed me down. I could've been very awkward and uncomfortable, but he really made me feel very much at ease."

In the two-part mini-series *World War III* (1982), Hudson played a president of the United States who is faced with nuclear war. Most of the film's plot takes place in Alaska, where Cathy Lee Crosby and David Soul are military personnel trying to nip the potential war in the bud, while Rock has his finger on the detonation button. Hudson's character, President McKenna, is a bachelor. When he is asked by newspaperwoman Dorothy Longworth (Katherine Helmond) about his "available" marital status, Rock answers, "I've reached that age where sex is constantly on my mind but rarely on my agenda."

According to Hudson in the early 1980s, "I know I said I wouldn't do another series after *McMillan*. I meant it too." However, he signed to star in a projected show to eventually be called *The Devlin Connection*.

"I had to be talked into this one," he explained. "What I determined not to do was just another private eye or crime series. But it seemed to me that if we could do a show in which the accent was on the fun of solving a crime, on the lines of *The Thin Man* movies, then maybe we'd have something. And that was the idea of *The Devlin Connection*."

Four shows were filmed starring Hudson, and suddenly he had the first of his major health problems and required heart bypass surgery in November 1981. *The Devlin Connection* cast-member Herb Jefferson, Jr., was quoted as saying, "I was working with him that very day, and you would have thought he was going in for a simple shot. He had complained of chest pains and had already undergone a stress test, but he made out it was nothing. He was still working full tilt—and the next thing we heard, he was having a five-way bypass operation."

On November 2, 1981, Hudson underwent five and a half hours of open-heart surgery to bypass clogged valves. The operation consisted of taking a section of vein from Rock's leg and bypassing the faulty passages in his bloodstream.

Tom Clark served as Rock's spokesperson at this time and reported to the press, "We're lucky they caught it this early. The doctors said he could have had a fatal heart attack within a month. The operation was an unqualified success. His heart is functioning perfectly on its own with no signs of any complications.

"He came through the operation with flying colors," continued Clark. "There are no complications whatsoever. He's expected to remain in intensive care for at least two days, which is normal procedure, and then leave the hospital in about ten days to continue recovery at home. We expect to see him back at work filming his new TV series, *The Devlin Connection*, by January 1 [1982].

"He is a very lucky man. He complained about chest pains a few weeks ago, but the original tests proved negative. However, last Friday, the doctors performed an angiogram and discovered the faulty valves," explained Clark. "We watched the Rams-Detroit football game in his room. He didn't show the slightest concern about his operation. He kidded me because I'd taken the Lions at six and a half points—and the Rams won by seven. Liz Taylor sent a huge bouquet, then Carol Burnett called on Sunday, and he spent time chatting with her."

One month later Rock glowed. "I feel terrific. There are no problems and I am anxious to get back to work. That's all in the past. I don't look back. After I've done something, I press on. And that goes for the surgery as well."

Suddenly Hudson was conscious of his health, and two of his favorite habits: smoking and drinking. With regard to his alcohol consumption, he explained,

"I've never had a drinking problem, I just drank a lot—out of boredom, pressure, frustration. Then a couple of years ago, I thought, 'What on earth am I doing, drinking myself into oblivion? What kind of existence is that?' So I quit it. I'll have a couple of drinks now, but I don't slug it away anymore. It was disgusting. There's more to life than getting soused every night."

With regard to the smoking, he proclaimed, "I began seeing a hypnotist last night. I've never gone in for that sort of thing so I am a bit skeptical. But if I can get help, which I need to quit smoking, I'll go anywhere. I do sneak in a few puffs every day. I'm in a stress business. When I used to work a long day, say from six in the morning until two A.M. the next day, I'd be good for two packs. But I was never concerned with any of this. I used to say, 'Who cares?' I was always blessed with perfect health. If I had a hangover, I knew it would eventually go away. Now I'm limiting myself to one or two drinks. That's it."

After that, it was right back to work for Rock. Within two months of his surgery he was back in the saddle with *The Devlin Connection*. He was very excited about the show. "The story line is a humdinger!" he said. He played a retired naval intelligence officer with a lot of cash that he acquired from a successful private-detective agency. "Then," he explained, "to my chagrin, I discover that I have a son [Jack Scalia]. He was raised by his grandfather, who was a cop, and now the son is in the private-eye business too. But he's inexperienced. So in spite of myself, I go out and help him. It's real life, in a sense."

However, the series was plagued with problems from the very start. The show didn't premier until October 2, 1982, and it was a total bomb. Explained

Rock before the opening episode was aired, "We
have thirteen shows done. Nine are usable . . . four
are not. We got off on the wrong foot. They just
weren't comedic. It was just another crime show.
Who cares? We want to show the fun of it, not the
who-did-it." Unfortunately nobody cared. When the
show was canceled, after all thirteen episodes were
aired, Hudson breathed a sigh of relief, admitting,
"That series undid me. When it was canceled, I was
overjoyed. It didn't have the comedy spark. It was
just another TV show. I was working in mediocrity.
That's what I didn't like. It was making me mediocre."

In November 1983, Rock Hudson and Robert
Mitchum flew to Tel Aviv, Israel, to begin filming
what was to be Rock's last movie role. The movie
also stars Ellen Burstyn as the wife of the ambassador (Mitchum). Rock and the cast reportedly all hated
the food in Israel, and *People* magazine ran photos of
Hudson tasting a batch of Mitchum's favorite recipe:
"Honest-to-God chili," which Mitchum whipped up
to sustain to two men during the Middle East shooting schedule. Never released theatrically, *The Ambassador* made its broadcast debut on cable television
in January of 1986.

Explaining his role in *The Ambassador*, Hudson reported that his part was "sort of a CIA-security
enigma, and I keep calling in to somebody, I don't
know who!"

After seeing the life-style in Israel, Hudson commented with disdain, "It was an unusual location for
a movie, but very enlightening. Soldiers with machine guns were all over the streets. You were constantly reminded of war and how people get used to
war. I think they should become more aware of the
stupidity of war."

Right after that he headed for Las Vegas to film
what was to be his final made-for-TV movie, *The*

Vegas Strip War. In the film he plays a casino owner who is in competition with another casino owner he is trying to get even with. "The title tells you the whole story, doesn't it? It's ridiculous," said Hudson, who joked about the forgettable film. "I own a casino—doesn't everybody?"

On March 31, 1984, Rock was saluted by the Actors' Fund of America at a fund-raising gala held at the Sands Hotel in Atlantic City, New Jersey. At the tribute Susan Saint James proclaimed that it was Hudson who had taught her "the art of good manners . . . He was never late for work, always knows his lines. You'd be surprised how many stars don't have those qualities."

Said Morgan Fairchild, "He's the epitome of what a movie star should be."

When it was Rock's turn to speak, he talked about the acting profession, stating, "Today, people think of us as normal folk who lead respectable lives, send their children to school just like everyone else. And once in a while, one or two of us have even got as far as running for public office."

It was reported that Rock Hudson was first diagnosed as having AIDS in June 1984. He kept it a secret from everyone around him. However, throughout 1984 he had been losing weight. When it began, it could easily be attributed to dieting and his own desire to trim up his physique, but as the year wore on, and more and more weight disappeared, he simply explained, "I have the energy of a teenager. I went to Israel last November for ten weeks, and when I tell you the food is inedible . . ." For the time being, his friends accepted that as a logical explanation.

In August 1984, a thin but determined Rock Hudson announced, "I would love to do a good play . . . or a good film. I'd love to do a good mini-series . . . Last year I didn't work for a year. That was okay. I like to work. I also like not to work. I like to bum around. I'm busier when I'm not working. Stuff to do around this house . . . gardening. I'm giving myself a breather. I'm storing up batteries again, till I can plunge in, plunge ahead."

An ABC-TV press release dated October 9, 1984, heralded the announcement that Rock Hudson would join the cast of the top-rated and most-talked-about television series of the decade: *Dynasty*. Filming of his ten episodes of the show began in late October, and his initial episode was broadcast in December, right before Christmas.

In the plot of the show, Rock plays Daniel Reece, the owner of Delta Rho Stables. Krystle Carrington (Linda Evans) is seeking her independence during a particularly troubled period in her marriage to the overpowering Blake Carrington (John Forsythe). She is interested in horse breeding, and with Daniel's encouragement, she begins spending a considerable amount of time at the stables. Daniel is an old buddy of Dex Dexter's (Michael Nader), and together they have gone on many undercover rescue missions. As the season progressed in early 1985, Krystle was contemplating having an affair with Daniel, who had dated her sister, but secretly always loved her.

At one point in the plot, Krystle and Daniel are alone together, and after she has been thrown to the ground by her horse, he ends up on top of her in a passionate embrace. Their kiss was later to become front-page news, when Rock Hudson's health record was disclosed.

Toward the end of the season, Daniel and Blake find themselves on an airplane together, and when they begin to fight, the plane goes out of control and crashes. Blake's son-in-law Jeff Colby (John James) rescues the men from the wreckage of the plane, and they return unscathed to Denver. Krystle is forced

to make a decision about her marriage and her at-
traction to Daniel. Krystle announces to Daniel that
she has chosen Blake, but there is a secret that she
wants to let him in on: he is the father of her niece,
Sammy Jo (Heather Locklear). Daniel and Krystle
travel to Sammy Jo's New York City apartment,
where he confronts her about her scandalous be-
havior. Says Sammy Jo, "Who do you think you are,
my father?"

Daniel is called away to join Dex on one of his
death-defying missions. Dex returns, Daniel does not,
and Sammy Jo inherits Daniel's wealth. His ten episodes of *Dynasty* were to be Rock Hudson's final
acting assignment.

When Rock Hudson arrived on the set of *Dynasty*
in October 1984, rumors began to circulate in show-
business circles about how horrible he looked. When
his first episode aired on December 19, 1984, millions of Rock's fans were tipped off to the fact that
something was wrong. His once-sparkling eyes were
eerie sunken orbs, there were deep pits in his once-
full cheeks, and any glance at his wrists or ankles
revealed a skeletal boniness.

In *U.S.A. Today* Rock retorted, "What sudden weight
loss? That's stupid . . . It took me a year to do it. It
was about time. I just took the challenge and went at
it." This was clearly not the result of any diet, something was frighteningly wrong with his health, and
the ultimate news was to turn Hollywood upside
down.

In one of his final press interviews, he pondered,
"Regrets? Oh, I have a few. I wanted a family. I
didn't have one. I wanted to sail around the world in
a big ketch I owned, but I was always too busy. I
wanted to direct a movie, but I never got the chance.
Besides, I don't think I could act and direct at the

same time. I was never good at doing two things at once. But I had a lot of fun along the way. I found a few friends." Rock Hudson was about to find out who his real friends were.

> "I don't know about you, but I'm not
> ready to die yet!"
> —Rock Hudson
> to John Forsythe
> in *Dynasty* (1985)

★ 8 ★
HOLLYWOOD GIBRALTAR
(JULY–OCTOBER 1985)

ON JULY 25, 1985, a friend and appointed spokesperson for Rock Hudson faced reporters outside the
American Hospital in Paris and announced to the
world, "Mr. Rock Hudson has Acquired Immune
Deficiency Syndrome (AIDS) which was diagnosed
in the U.S. He came to Paris to consult with a specialist in this disease," said Yanou Collart.

With that announcement, Rock Hudson's homosexuality and, as it was being called, "the gay plague"
became headline news. Suddenly AIDS wasn't just
an illness affecting an underworld element of society, and Rock Hudson wasn't just a movie actor.

Collart's statement continued, "Prior to meeting
the specialist, he became very ill at the Ritz Hotel.
His personal business manager, Mark Miller, advised
him from California to enter the American Hospital
immediately. The physicians discovered abnormalities in the liver that, without knowledge of an AIDS
diagnosis, were suspected to be caused either by in-
fections or were consistent with metastatic [cancerous]
liver disease. These abnormalities are currently being
evaluated." The publicist finished with the statement,
"He doesn't have any idea now how he contracted
AIDS."

A hospital spokesman named Bruce Rador confirmed that the disclosure of Hudson's condition was not the hospital's action. "All this AIDS stuff is [from] Rock Hudson and his people. It is a secret what our doctors are doing here. It is not French tradition to talk about patients."

It was learned that Hudson suddenly left for Paris in order to be treated with the experimental drug HPA-23. It was later acknowledged that this was not Hudson's first pilgrimage to Paris for HPA-23 treatment. He had in fact been administered the drug several times in the past thirteen months, knowing that he was dying of the dreaded illness. The first instance had occurred the year before, when he re-routed himself through Paris, having attended a retrospective festival of his films in Deauville.

Hudson himself was never to admit publicly to any homosexual act, interest, or life-style. Only weeks before the press conference Hudson had stated in an interview, "I like to keep my secrets to myself, and I guess they will die with me." It seems that Hudson in reality would have preferred it all left this way: a secret.

However, gay activist Armistead Maupin, who was formerly a columnist on the *San Francisco Chronicle*, volunteered the information in the July 25, 1985, issue of that newspaper that he had once approached Rock about publicly announcing his homosexuality. Said Maupin, "Rock seemed to take to the idea and said, 'One of these days I'm going to have a lot to tell.' I thought it would be a good idea, because he was actually the same in private life as on the screen: very masculine and natural. You could see the idea would be difficult for some men of his generation—he could never bring himself to go public about it."

Continued Maupin, "Rock had learned the lesson well in Hollywood. He played by the rules. These rules say that you keep quiet about being gay and everyone will lie about it for you. The gossip columnists will make up girlfriends for you and everyone in Hollywood will know you are gay except the public."

In the same issue of the newspaper, another gay friend of Hudson's, Ken Maley, announced, "Rock loved San Francisco and was coming here for years. We never went out to gay places with Rock in L.A., but in San Francisco it was different—he was more relaxed about it." The article also named several gay clubs that Hudson frequented: the Trockadero Transfer and the I-Beam.

It was Maley who spoke about Hudson's wedding to Phyllis Gates, stating, "The studio arranged the whole wedding, the publicity, the honeymoon, everything. He frequently said he was bitter about it. That was in the days when the studio ran the stars' lives." Admitted several insiders, "We all knew, but what did it matter?"

That was all the encouragement that the tabloids needed. Suddenly Hudson's private life was anything but private: "Rock Hudson's Tragic Battle for Life" (*Star*, August 6, 1985), "The Man Who Led Rock Astray" (*Globe*, August 20, 1985), "Rock Hudson: The REAL Story" (*National Enquirer*, October 22, 1985), "The Dramatic Last-Ditch Attempt to Save Rock's Life" (*National Enquirer* October 15, 1985), "Rock's Tragic Last Plea" (*Globe*, October 22, 1985), even the tawdry "Pathetic Deathbed Confession by Superstar's Ex-Lover . . . I KILLED ROCK HUDSON" (*National Examiner*, October 29, 1985). When *People* magazine published the first of its three 1985 Hudson cover stories, "The Other Life of Rock Hudson" (August 12), it became the largest-selling issue in the magazine's history.

On July 30, 1985, at the cost of $250,000, Rock Hudson chartered an Air France 747 "Jumbo Jet" and returned to Los Angeles. The *New York Post*, among other papers, published the photo of Hudson leaving the plane on a stretcher, the out-of-focus work of a telephoto camera lens. Rock's illness was the story of the year, and never before in his career had he garnered so much publicity.

Said his publicist, Dale Olson, "it has been his [Hudson's] desire that if he can do anything at all to help the rest of humanity by his acknowledging that he has this disease, he will be happy to do that. It is his desire that if he has this deadly disease, he acknowledges it so that it might help the rest of the world and create more research toward finding a cure."

Hudson was immediately taken to the UCLA Medical Center for tests and treatment. On the evening of August 24, 1985, Hudson was released from the medical center and taken to his home. Victor Mitry, spokesman for the hospital, said of Rock, "His overall medical condition has improved slightly since his admission July 30. His condition was fair at the time of his discharge. He will require ongoing medical care at home."

For the next month and a half, the atmosphere in Rock's Los Angeles home, in the Coldwater Canyon vicinity, was reminiscent of a three-ring circus. While Hudson lay in bed heavily sedated and, by many reports, completely unaware of what was going on around him, his former intimates were busy battling for control of the Hudson household.

The cast of characters who would form the literal soap opera of Rock Hudson's last days seemed to be growing. The scenario included Mark Miller (secretary), Dale Olson (publicist), Marc Christian (live-in lover), Ross Hunter (friend and producer), and last but not least . . . the return of former "companion" Tom Clark.

Tom Clark had been missing from Rock's life since an argument in November 1983. One inside source recalls being in New Orleans in mid-1983 when Ross Hunter was directing a play entitled *Breaking Up the Act*, which starred Evelyn Keyes and Jan Sterling. After several drinks, Clark announced that he was Hudson's "lover" at the time. The source surmises that Clark's pronouncements rubbed Hudson the wrong way. Hudson was not thrilled by someone making such public statements, and the two men hadn't spoken in almost two years.

When Clark returned to Los Angeles, he is said to have taken over the running of Hudson's home, which included throwing current live-in lover Marc Christian out, forcing the rarely employed thirty-two-year-old blond out of the house. Christian, who refused to leave the property, was to take up residence in Hudson's guest house, to make room for the nursing staff. Christian paints a picture of himself as a concerned benevolent soul, while other members of the Hudson inner circle have called him "a common street hustler" (*People*, November 25, 1985).

Rock's illness left him weak. Several of his lifelong friends came to visit. Tony Perkins, Claire Trevor, Carol Burnett, and Elizabeth Taylor came to see him at the UCLA Medical Center. Another dear friend, Roddy McDowell, was so visibly distressed during one visit to Hudson's house that Mark Miller told him not to come back until he got a grip on himself and could see Rock with more buoyant spirits. Rock reportedly commented, "Some days, I can't wait for the next visitors. The next day, I wish people would go away and leave me alone." Ross Hunter claimed that "I was with him just about every day." The group living at the house stated that he was "hardly ever" there.

In early September 1985, it was announced that

Rock Hudson was writing his autobiography, with the six-figure advance monies going toward AIDS research. In 1982 Hudson irrevocably dismissed ever writing an autobiography by commenting, "What do I want people to know about me? Nothing. It's none of their business. As far as correcting misconceptions, good luck!" Why would he suddenly change this decision? According to several reports, Hudson was in such a debilitated state his last month that he didn't have any idea what was going on around him.

According to Ross Hunter, "Rock was a very private person. I just can't believe he would have wanted a book like this. Rock was my friend. I made eleven movies with him, and he never discussed his personal life. In my wildest dreams, I couldn't see him writing this."

Argued Hudson's attorney, Paul Sherman, "I don't know why Ross Hunter is doing this. But I can tell you Rock wanted this book. All of the funds he would have gotten will go to AIDS research. Why Hunter would want to damage that, I don't know."

Said writer Sara Davidson, "I met with Rock Hudson in his home on numerous occasions. We did formal interviews and made tape recordings. He gave me as much time as his health permitted."

On September 19, 1985, at the Westin Bonaventure Hotel in Los Angeles, a gala fund-raising benefit was held, producing a million dollars for AIDS research. Carol Burnett and Sammy Davis, Jr., performed a medley of show tunes, and Cyndi Lauper and Rod Stewart performed the song "Time After Time" together. Elizabeth Taylor was the hostess of the evening. Burt Reynolds read a message from President Reagan that called for Americans to "reflect conscientiously on their responsibility to do whatever is in their power to ensure that this pernicious syndrome [AIDS] is halted in its tracks and ultimately cured."

Linda Evans introduced Burt Lancaster, who read a statement from Rock Hudson. It read: "I regret the circumstances of which you are all aware that prevent me from being with you tonight. People have told me that the disclosure [his admission of AIDS infection] helped to make this evening an immediate sellout. I have also been told . . . my own situation has brought enormous international attention to the gravity of this disease . . . and is leading to more research, more contribution of funds, and a better understanding of this disease." And finally the magnanimous, "I am not happy that I am sick. I am not happy that I have AIDS, but if that is helping others, I can, at least, know that my own misfortune has had some positive worth."

Meanwhile, back at the Hudson camp, the infighting continued when Ross Hunter claimed that Rock had nothing to do with the aforementioned statement. Argued Dale Olson, "It was approved by Rock Hudson and released. He was lucid and understood every word." At this point what difference did it make whether Hudson sat up and composed every word of the statement or simply approved of the statement? While his friends carried on petty arguments, Rock Hudson was dying of an illness of unspeakable horror.

Although it was said that Rock considered himself an atheist, he had been born a Roman Catholic, and on September 25, a priest paid him a visit. He took Communion and was issued last rites. One woman stood vigil outside the gates of Rock's house, and on the night of October 1, a Pentecostal prayer group, including Pat and Shirley Boone, visited. Said Pat Boone, "For Shirley and I, there had been a sense of being involved from a distance. We believed that even though there was no medical hope for him, we had a deep spiritual concern and felt that this might lead to a physical answer as well." It was reported that on the day he died, Shirley Boone again came into the house, went straight to Rock's deathbed, and began chanting, "Get the disease out of the body," and then was heard speaking in tongues.

Was Rock Hudson aware of the visitors he had the last two weeks of his life? Did he want Marc Christian thrown out of his house? Did he approve of the "autobiography" about his life? Did he have any idea of the impact that his AIDS announcement caused? Did he know about the San Francisco attempts to make him a gay cult hero? How would he feel about being pronounced by *Time* magazine as "the most famous homosexual in the world"? Would he ever have wanted his death to become such a public event? On October 2, 1985, the answers to all of these questions died with him.

"Dear God—is this the way it's going to be?"

—Rock Hudson
in *The Martian Chronicles* (1980)

★ 9 ★
TARNISHED ANGELS

ROCK HUDSON was a consummate superstar. He appeared in sixty-five movies, three television series, four TV mini-series, two made-for-TV movies, six theatrical productions, and recorded one record album. He was never responsible for any production delays, never had a breakdown or an addiction, was never once quoted as saying one disparaging thing about another living human being, and was never accused of any thought, word, or deed that in any way would consciously harm anyone. He conducted himself as a perfect gentleman at all times. Yet when he died at the age of fifty-nine, the vultures were already circling overhead.

According to his expressly written wishes, upon his death, his remains were cremated. Also, following his instructions, on October 19, 1985, one hundred and fifty of his closest friends were to gather and have a party in his honor rather than a mourning memorial. According to publicist Yanou Collart, "He doesn't want anybody to be sad. He wants everybody to be happy because he had a good life. Rock loved parties. He's left orders to have champagne, caviar, and Mariachi bands." Present at the last party were Elizabeth Taylor, Carol Burnett, Angie Dickinson, Ricardo Montalban, Glenn Ford, Tab Hunter, Roddy McDowell, Jessica Walter, Lee Remick, Robert Wagner, Stefanie Powers, Esther Williams, Susan Saint James, Jane Withers, Dale Olson, and Martha Raye.

According to Elizabeth Taylor's publicist, Chen Sam, "It was friends getting together. Whoever felt like it got up and expressed their feelings and wonderful anecdotes about him. Most people got up and said something. These were people who were his friends, who had worked with him. They each recalled a specific memory of him." Mexican food and margaritas, which were Rock's favorite cuisine, and cocktail were served. It was instructed by Rock's will that his ashes were to be scattered in the Pacific Ocean, near Catalina Island, the following day.

Naturally there were the crasser moments that day. Press helicopters buzzed over the late actor's estate, and it was noted in the *Washington Post* that one of Hudson's neighbors was charging reporters three hundred dollars for the rights to stand on her property to observe the celebrity mourners.

Tributes came from several of his close friends in show business. "I love him and he's tragically gone," said Elizabeth Taylor. "Please God, he has not died in vain."

A lot of vicious gossip circulated after Rock's AIDS disclosure concerning the kissing scenes that he and Linda Evans performed on *Dynasty*. Yet in spite of all of the rumors of "turmoil" on the TV show's set, Evans's comments were totally compassionate. "As fine an actor as Rock Hudson was, and as much as he shared his craft with us, I feel his greatest gift to the world was in his acknowledgment of his disease and in his willingness to educate people and raise their consciousness," Linda said, adding, "His death is a great loss to all of us, but his legacy will be our continued fight for a cure for AIDS."

Doris Day, his famous comedy costar, said, "Oh,

my God. What can I say? This is where our faith is really tested. It's so terrible I can't believe it. All those years of working with him, I saw him as big, healthy, and indestructible. I'm saddened by this and all I can do is uplift my thinking. Life is eternal, and I hope we meet again. We had such a special relationship and a special humor that we shared. Working with him was unlike working with anyone else. It was so wonderful."

President Ronald Reagan issued this statement: "Nancy and I are saddened by the news of Rock Hudson's death. He will always be remembered for his dynamic impact on the film industry, and fans all over the world will certainly mourn his loss. He will be remembered for his humanity, his sympathetic and well-deserved reputation for kindness. May God rest his soul."

Said Jane Wyman, "Rock was a dear friend for over thirty years. He had a great talent, and all of us who worked with him will miss him terribly."

According to Burt Reynolds, "It's the end of an era when a movie star really looked like a movie star. Rock was six-feet-four, incredibly handsome, and proved with *Giant* and *Pillow Talk* his unbelievable versatility. I never knew anyone who didn't like him."

"He was a very special human being," said Jane Withers. "Everybody that knew him loved him. We spent a year together making *Giant,* and it was one of the nicest experiences of my life, and he was a very special friend. He'll be missed by the world and especially by me."

It was revealed after his death that the FBI maintained a file on Rock Hudson's sex life. Among other things, the file stated that "it was common knowledge in the motion picture industry that Rock Hudson was suspected of having homosexual tendencies." The dossier also featured the information that "Rock Hudson has not been the subject of an FBI investigation. During 1965, however, a confidential informant reported that several years ago while he was in New York he had an 'affair' with movie star Rock Hudson." However, it admitted, "The fingerprint files of the Identification Division of the FBI contain no arrest data identifiable with Mr. Hudson based upon background information submitted in connection with this name check."

Apparently the file was the result of an incident that happened in 1965 when Rock Hudson arrived unannounced at President Lyndon Johnson's ranch, via private plane. He was accompanied by "an alleged homosexual," and the two of them "requested a meeting with Mrs. [Lady Bird] Johnson and a tour of the ranch. However, she did not meet with them upon our advice and they departed a short time later." The file was compiled after the incident in the "protective interest" of the "First Family."

Rock's property, including his Beverly Hills home and a Manhattan apartment on Central Park West, is to be sold, with the money generated by the sales to be donated to AIDS research. The two-bedroom bachelor home that he lived in and later shared with Phyllis Gates was purchased by Gates just prior to his death. Although she never spoke to him after their divorce, she bore him no ill will.

However, when Rock Hudson's will was read, some more ugliness surfaced in the form of a $14 million lawsuit filed by Rock's embittered boyfriend Marc Christian, who is represented by lawyer Marvin Mitchelson. The allegation is that Hudson knew he had AIDS and continued to have sex with Christian without informing Christian of his illness, and thus potentially endangering his life. Said Mitchelson, "These two people lived together and shared the bedroom. Rock Hudson was not only fond of this man, but told him in love letters he was the most important person in his life. Whether a person is a hustler or not—my client isn't—they have a right to know if they are being exposed to a life-threatening disease." It is debated whether or not Christian has a valid case, and whether disclosure of exposure to AIDS is a matter of courtesy, or of law.

"Rock tried to get rid of him, but couldn't," alleged the *New York Post.* If Christian continued to have sex with Hudson from June 1984–June 1985 while the actor's body disintegrated so dramatically, wasn't he suspicious of the disease, suspicious enough to abstain? Several informants claim to have had sex with Rock Hudson during the last two years of his life.

The bulk of Rock's estate, estimated at $27 million, went to Mark Miller and George Nader. Tom Clark was written out of the will when it was amended on August 23, 1984. Marc Christian claims, "Guilt is what prompted Rock to leave most of his estate to George Nader." Marc Christian received nothing.

According to Yanou Collart, "The hardest thing I ever had to do in my life was to walk into his room and read him the press release," she said of her task in July of 1985. "I'll never forget the look on his face. How can I explain it? Very few people knew he was gay. In his eyes was the realization that he was destroying his own image. After I read it, he said simply, 'That's it, it has to be done.' " If Rock Hudson was not conscious of another moment of his life after that, did it really matter? Wasn't his action of selflessly throwing his entire career image away in the hope that someone else—anyone else—might benefit, enough of a sacrifice to demonstrate what kind of a person he truly was?

Rock Hudson has left a legacy of sixty-five movies and countless hours of film. That made him a movie star. Rock Hudson gave up the only thing that he held valuable to him: his privacy. That made him a hero more admirable than any Hollywood script he delivered a line of "on camera." He was always someone to look up to in the movies; now he will be remembered as a man more worthy of praise than any role he ever portrayed on the screen.

ROCK HUDSON

FILMOGRAPHY

(1) Fighter Squadron
Warner Brothers (1948) color/96 minutes
Producer . . . . Seton I. Miller
Director . . . . Raoul Walsh
Screenplay . . . . Seton I. Miller

Cast:

Major Ed Hardin . . . . Edmond O'Brien
Captain Stu Hamilton . . . Robert Stack
Colonel Bill Brickley . . . . . John Rodney
Sergeant Dolan . . . . Tom D'Andrea
Brigadier General Mike
    McCready . . . . Henry Hull
Tennessee . . . . James Holden
Captain Duke Chappell . . Walter Reed
Brigadier General M.
    Gilbert . . . . Shepperd Strudwick
Lieutenants . . . . Don Phillips
. . . . ROCK HUDSON

(2) Undertow
Universal (1949) black & white/71 minutes
Producer . . . . William Castle
Director . . . . William Castle
Screenplay . . . . Arthur T. Horman

Cast:

Tony Reagan . . . . Scott Brady
Danny Morgan . . . . John Russell

Sally Lee .... Dorothy Hart
Ann McKnight .... Peggy Dow
Cooper .... Charles Sherlock
Fisher .... Robert Easton
Reckling .... Bruce Bennett
Frost .... Gregg Martell
Stoner .... Robert Anderson
Detective .... ROCK HUDSON

(3) I Was a Shoplifter
Universal (1950) black & white/74 minutes
Producer .... Leonard Goldstein
Director .... Charles Lamont
Screenplay .... Irwin Gielgud

Cast:

Jeff Andrews .... Scott Brady
Faye Burton .... Mona Freeman
Ina Perdue .... Andrea King
Pepe .... Anthony (Tony) Curtis
Herb Klaxton .... Charles Drake
The Champ .... Gregg Martell
Harry Dunson .... Larry Keating
Barkie Neff .... Robert Gist
Sheriff Bascom .... Michael Raffetto
Store Detective .... ROCK HUDSON
Aunt Clara .... Nana Bryant

(4) One Way Street
Universal (1950) black & white/79 minutes
Producer .... Leonard Goldstein
Director .... Hugo Fregonese
Screenplay .... Lawrence Kimble
    —based on the novel *Death on a Side Street* by
    Lawrence Kimble

Cast:

Doc Matson .... James Mason
Laura .... Marta Toren
Wheeler .... Dan Duryea
Ollie .... William Conrad
Grieder .... King Donovan

Arnie ....Jack Elam
Hank Torres...........Tito Renaldo
Father Moreno.........Basil Ruysdael
Francisco Morales ....Rudolpho Acosta
Truck Driver ....ROCK HUDSON

(5) **Winchester '73***
Universal (1950) black & white/92 minutes
Producer ....Aaron Rosenberg
Director ....Anthony Mann
Screenplay.............Robert L. Richards
—based on the story "Winchester '73" by Stuart
N. Lake

Cast:

Lin McAdam ....James Stewart
Lola Manners ....Shelley Winters
Waco Johnny Dean .....Dan Duryea
Dutch Henry Brown.....Stephen McNally
"High Spade" Frankie
    Wilson ....Millard Mitchell
Steve Miller.............Charles Drake
Joe Lamonte ....John McIntire
Wyatt Earp ....Will Geer
Sergeant Wilkes ....Jay C. Flippen
Young Bull ....ROCK HUDSON
Doan..................Anthony (Tony) Curtis

(6) **Peggy**
Universal (1950) color/77 minutes
Producer ....Ralph Dietrich
Director ....Frederick de Cordova
Screenplay.............George F. Slaven
Story ....Leon Ware

Cast:

Peggy Brookfield........Diana Lynn
Professor Brookfield.....Charles Coburn
Mrs. Emelia Fielding ....Charlotte Greenwood

---

*available on videocassette

Susan Brookfield	Barbara Lawrence
Tom Fielding	Charles Drake
Johnny Higgins	ROCK HUDSON
Miss Zim	Connie Gilchrist
Dr. Wilcox	Griff Barnett
Charles Trowbridge	Dean Stockwell
Mrs. Privet	Ellen Corby

(7) **The Desert Hawk**
Universal (1950) color/77½ minutes
Producer ....Leonard Goldstein
Director ....Frederick de Cordova
Screenplay............Aubrey Wisberg,
    Jack Pollexfen, and Gerald Drayson Adams

Cast:

Princess Shaharazade	Yvonne De Carlo
Omar	Richard Greene
Aladdin	Jackie Gleason
Prince Murad	George Macready
Kibar	Carl Esmond
Samad	Marc Lawrence
Undine	Lucille Barkley
Yasmin	Anne Pearce
Maznah	Lois Andrews
Captain Ras	ROCK HUDSON

(8) **Shakedown**
Universal (1950) black & white/80 minutes
Producer ....Ted Richmond
Director ....Joseph Pevney
Screenplay.............Alfred Lewis Levitt
—based on the novel *Shakedown* by Nat Dallinger
    and Don Martin

Cast:

Jack Early	Howard Duff
Ellen Bennett	Peggy Dow
Nick Palmer	Brian Donlevy
David Glover	Bruce Bennett
Nightclub hatcheck girl	Peggy Castle
Nita Palmer	Anne Vernon
Harry Colton	Lawrence Tierney
Nightclub doorman	ROCK HUDSON

(9) **Tomahawk**
Universal (1951) color/90 minutes
Producer ....Leonard Goldstein
Director ....George Sherman
Screenplay..............Silvia Richards
               and Maurice Geraghty
Story ....Daniel Jarrett

Cast:

Jim Bridger.............Van Heflin
Julie Madden ....Yvonne De Carlo
Colonel Carrington ......Preston Foster
Sol Beckworth ....Jack Oakie
Lieutenant Bob Dancy ...Alex Nicol
Dan Castello ....Tom Tully
Mrs. Carrington.........Ann Doran
Burt Hanna ....ROCK HUDSON
Monahseetah ....Susan Cabot
Captain Fetterman ......Arthur Space

(10) **Air Cadet**
Universal (1951) black & white/94 minutes
Producer ....Aaron Rosenberg
Director ....Joseph Pevney
Screenplay..............Robert I. Richards
Story ....Robert Soderberg
               and Robert I. Richards

Cast:

Major Jack Page.........Stephen McNally
Janet Page..............Gail Russell
Joe Czanoczek ....Alex Nicol
Russ Coulter ....Richard Long
Captain Sullivan........Charles Drake
Upper Classman ....ROCK HUDSON
Walt Carver ....Robert Authur
Pat.....................Peggie Castle
Jerry Connell ....James Best
Instructor ....Russell Dennis

(11) **The Fat Man**
Universal (1951) black & white/77½ minutes
Producer . . . . Aubrey Schenck
Director . . . . William Castle
Screenplay . . . . Harry Essex
and Leonard Lee
Story . . . . Leonard Lee

Cast:

Brad Runyan . . . . J. Scott Smart
Pat Boyd . . . . Julie London
Roy Clark . . . . ROCK HUDSON
Bill Norton . . . . Clinton Sundberg
Jane Adams . . . . Jayne Meadows
Gene Gordon . . . . John Russell
Detective Stark . . . . Jerome Cowan
Ed Deets . . . . Emmett Kelly
Lola Gordon . . . . Lucille Barkley
Shifty . . . . Teddy Hart

(12) **Iron Man**
Universal (1951) black & white/82 minutes
Producer . . . . Aaron Rosenberg
Director . . . . Joseph Pevney
Screenplay . . . . George Zuckerman
and Bordon Chase
Story . . . . William R. Burnett

Cast:

Coke Mason . . . . Jeff Chandler
Rose Warren . . . . Evelyn Keyes
George Mason . . . . Stephen McNally
Tiny . . . . Joyce Holden
Speed O'Keefe . . . . ROCK HUDSON
Max Watkins . . . . Jim Backus
Alex . . . . Jim Arness
Pete . . . . Paul Javor
Joe Savella . . . . Steve Martin
Jackie Bowden . . . . Eddie Simms

(13) **Bright Victory**
Universal (1951) black & white/97 minutes
Producer ....Robert Buckner
Director ....Mark Robson
Screenplay..............Robert Buckner
—based on the novel *Lights Out* by Bayard Kendrick

Cast:

Larry Nevins............Arthur Kennedy
Judy Greene ....Peggy Dow
Chris Paterson ....Julia Adams
Joe Morgan.............James Edwards
Mr. Nevins ....Will Geer
Mr. Paterson............Minor Watson
Bill Grayson ....Jim Backus
Janet Grayson...........Joan Banks
Mrs. Nevins.............Nana Bryant
Sergeant John Masterson Richard Egan
Corporal John Flagg.....ROCK HUDSON

(14) **Here Come the Nelsons**
(also known as *"Meet the Nelsons"*)
Universal (1952) black & white/76 minutes
Producer ....Aaron Rosenberg
Director ....Frederick de Cordova
Screenplay..............Ozzie Nelson,
            Donald Nelson, and William Davenport

Cast:

Ozzie...................Ozzie Nelson
Harriet.................Harriet Nelson
Ricky...................Ricky Nelson
David ....David Nelson
Charles Jones ....ROCK HUDSON
Barbara ....Barbara Lawrence
Duke...................Shelton Leonard
Joe Randolph ....Jim Backus
S. T. Jones ....Paul Harvey
H. J. Bellows...........Gale Gordon

(15) **Bend of the River***
Universal (1952) color/91 minutes
Producer .... Aaron Rosenberg
Director .... Anthony Mann
Screenplay .... Borden Chase
—based on the novel *Bend of the Snake* by
William Gulick

Cast:

Glyn McLyntock .... James Stewart
Cole Garett .... Arthur Kennedy
Laura Baile .... Julia Adams
Trey Wilson .... ROCK HUDSON
Marjie Baile .... Lori Nelson
Jeremy Baile .... Jay C. Flippen
Shorty................. Henry "Harry" Morgan
Captain Mello .... Chubby Johnson
Long Tom.............. Royal Dano
Tom Hendricks .... Howard Petrie

(16) **Scarlet Angel**
Universal (1952) color/81 minutes
Producer .... Leonard Goldstein
Director .... Sidney Salkow
Screenplay.............. Oscar Brodney

Cast:

Roxy McClanahan .... Yvonne De Carlo
Frank Truscott.......... ROCK HUDSON
Malcolm Bradley .... Richard Denning
Linda Caldwell .... Bodil Miller
Susan Bradley .... Amanda Blake
Morgan Caldwell .... Henry O'Neill
Pierre .... Henry Brandon
Eugenia Caldwell .... Maude Wallace
Walter Frisby .... Dan Riss
Gus .... George Hamilton

(17) **Has Anybody Seen My Gal?**
Universal (1952) color/89 minutes
Producer .... Ted Richmond
Director .... Douglas Sirk

*available on videocassette

Screenplay . . . . Samuel Hoffman
Story . . . . Elanor H. Porter

Cast:

Millicent . . . . Piper Laurie
Dan . . . . ROCK HUDSON
Samuel Fulton . . . . Charles Coburn
Roberta . . . . Gigi Perreau
Harriet Blaisdell . . . . Lynn Bari
Charles Blaisdell . . . . Larry Gates
Howard . . . . William Reynolds
Carl Pennock . . . . Skip Homeier
Judge Wilkins . . . . Paul Harvey
Mr. Norton . . . . Frank Ferguson
Youth . . . . James Dean

(18) **Horizons West**
Universal (1952) color/81 minutes
Producer . . . . Albert J. Cohen
Director . . . . Budd Boetticher
Screenplay . . . . Louis Stevens

Cast:

Dan Hammond . . . . Robert Ryan
Lorna Hardin . . . . Julia Adams
Neal Hammond . . . . ROCK HUDSON
Ira Hammond . . . . John McIntire
Sally . . . . Judith Braun
Cord Hardin . . . . Raymond Burr
Tiny . . . . James Arness
Martha Hammond . . . . . . Frances Bavier
Dandy Taylor . . . . Dennis Weaver
Frank Tarleton . . . . Tom Powers

(19) **The Lawless Breed**
Universal (1952) color/83 minutes
Producer . . . . William Alland
Director . . . . Raoul Walsh
Screenplay . . . . Bernard Gordon
Story . . . . William Alland

Cast:

John Wesley Hardin . . . . . ROCK HUDSON
Rosie . . . . Julia Adams
J. C. Hardin/John
    Clements . . . . John McIntire
Jane Brown . . . . Mary Castle
Ike Hanley . . . . Hugh O'Brien
Zeke Jenkins . . . . Forrest Lewis
Dirk Hanley . . . . Lee Van Cleef
Chick Noonan . . . . Tom Fadden
Joe Hardin . . . . William Pullen
Jim Clements . . . . Dennis Weaver

(20) Seminole
Universal (1953) color/87 minutes
Producer . . . . Howard Christie
Director . . . . Budd Boetticher
Screenplay . . . . Charles K. Peck Jr.

Cast:

Lance Caldwell . . . . ROCK HUDSON
Revere Muldoon . . . . Barbara Hale
Osceola . . . . Anthony Quinn
Major Degan . . . . Richard Carlson
Kajeck . . . . Hugh O'Brien
Lieutenant Hamilton . . . . Russell Johnson
Sergeant Magruder . . . . . . Lee Marvin
Mulak . . . . Ralph Moody
Zachary Taylor . . . . Fay Roope
Corporal Gerad . . . . James Best

(21) Sea Devils*
RKO (1953) color/91 minutes
Producer . . . . David E. Rose
Director . . . . Raoul Walsh
Screenplay . . . . Borden Chase
   —suggested by the novel *Toilers of the Sea* by
    Victor Hugo

---

*available on videocassette

Cast:

Droucette . . . . Yvonne De Carlo
Gilliatt . . . . ROCK HUDSON
Rantaine . . . . Maxwell Reed
Lethierry . . . . Denis O'Dea
Ragan . . . . Michael Goodliffe
Willie . . . . Bryan Forbes
Fouche . . . . Jacques Brunius
Benson . . . . Ivor Barnard
Baron de Vaudrec . . . . Arthur Wontner
Napoleon . . . . Garard Oury

(22) Gun Fury
Columbia (1953) color/83 minutes
Producer . . . . Lewis J. Rachmil
Director . . . . Raoul Walsh
Screenplay . . . . Irving Wallace
and Roy Huggins
—based on the novel *Ten Against Caesar* by
Kathleen B. George and Robert A. Granger

Cast:

ROCK HUDSON
Donna Reed
Phil Carey
Lee Marvin
Neville Brand
Leo Gordon

—NOTE: Originally shown in 3-D

(23) The Golden Blade
Universal (1953) color/81 minutes
Producers . . . . Richard Wilson
and Leonard Goldstein
Director . . . . Nathan Juran
Screenplay . . . . John Rich

Cast:

Harun . . . . ROCK HUDOSN
Khairuman . . . . Piper Laurie

Hadi	Gene Evans
Jalar	George Macready
Barcus	Steven Geray
Caliph	Edgar Barrier
Handmaidens	Anita Ekberg
	Renate Huy
	Valerie Jackson
	Alice Kelley
Rabble Rouser	Dennis Weaver
Town Crier	Guy Williams

(24) Back to God's Country
Universal (1953) color/78 minutes
Producer .... Howard Christie
Director .... Joseph Pevney
Screenplay .... Tom Reed
—based on the novel *Back to God's Country* by James Oliver Curwood

Cast:

Peter Keith	ROCK HUDSON
Doris Keith	Marcia Henderson
Paul Blake	Steve Cochran
Frank Hudson	Hugh O'Brien
Shorter	Chubby Johnson
Fitzsimmons	Tudor Owen
Carstairs	Arthur Space
Lagi	Bill Radovich
Joe	John Cliff
Uppy	Pat Hogan

(25) Taza, Son of Cochise
Universal (1954) color/79 minutes
Producer .... Ross Hunter
Director .... Douglas Sirk
Screenplay .... Gerald Drayson Adams

Cast:

Taza	ROCK HUDSON
Oona	Barbara Rush
Captain Brunett	Gregg Palmer
Naiche	Bart Roberts

Grey Eagle .... Morris Ankrum
Geronimo .... Ian MacDonald
Sergeant Hamma........ Joe Sawyer
General Crook .... Robert Burton
Chato .... Eugene Iglesias
            and
Cochise................ Jeff Chandler

—NOTE: Originally shown in 3-D

(26) **Magnificent Obsession***
Universal (1954) color/108 minutes
Producer .... Ross Hunter
Director .... Douglas Sirk
Screenplay.............. Robert Blees
    —based on the novel *Magnificent Obsession* by
    Lloyd C. Douglas and screenplay by Sarah
    Y. Mason

Cast:

Helen Phillips .... Jane Wyman
Bob Merrick .... ROCK HUDSON
Nancy Ashford.......... Agnes Moorehead
Joyce Phillips .... Barbara Rush
Tom Masterson .... Gregg Palmer
Randolph............... Otto Kruger
Dr. Giraud .... Paul Cavanagh
Valerie .... Sara Shane
Dr. Dodge .... Richard H. Cutting
Judy .... Judy Nugent

(27) **Bengal Brigade**
Universal (1954) color/87 minutes
Producer .... Ted Richmond
Director ....,... Laslo Benedek
Screenplay.............. Seton I. Miller
    —based on the novel *Bengal Tiger* by Hall Hunter

---

*available on videocassette

Cast:

Captain Jeffrey
 Claybourne . . . . ROCK HUDSON
Vivian Morrow . . . . Arlene Dahl
Latah . . . . Ursula Thiess
Colonel Morrow . . . . Torin Thatcher
Rajah Karan . . . . Arnold Moss
Captain Ronald Blaine . . . Daniel O'Herlihy
Hari Lal . . . . Harold Gordon
Sergeant Major Furan
 Singh . . . . Michael Ansara
Mahindra . . . . Leonard Strong
Bulbir . . . . Shepard Menken

(28) **Captain Lightfoot**
Universal (1955) color/91 minutes
Producer . . . . Ross Hunter
Director . . . . Douglas Sirk
Screenplay . . . . W. R. Burnett
 —based on the novel *Captain Lightfoot* by W. R.
 Burnett

Cast:

Michael Martin (a/k/a
 Captain Lightfoot) . . . ROCK HUDSON
Aga Doherty . . . . Barbara Rush
John Doherty (a/k/a
 Captain Thunderbolt) Jeff Morrow
Callahan . . . . Finlay Currie
Lady Anne More . . . . Kathleen Ryan
Regis Donnell . . . . Denis O'Dea
Captain Hood . . . . Geoffrey Toone
Lord Glen . . . . Milton Edwards
Brady . . . . Henry Goldblatt
Dan Shanley . . . . Charles Fitzsimons

(29) **One Desire**
Universal (1955) color/94 minutes
Producer . . . . Ross Hunter
Director . . . . Jerry Hopper
Screenplay . . . . Lawrence Roman
 —based on the novel *Tacey Cromwell* by Conrad
 Richter

Cast:

Tacey Cromwell.........Anne Baxter
Clint Saunders.........ROCK HUDSON
Judith Watrous.........Julia Adams
Senator Watrous........Carl Benton Reid
Seely..................Natalie Wood
Mrs. O'Dell............Betty Garde
MacBain................William Hopper
Nugget.................Betty Curtis
Marjorie Huggins.......Adrienne Marden
Flo....................Fay Morley

(30) **All That Heaven Allows**
Universal (1955) color/89 minutes
Producer..............Ross Hunter
Director..............Douglas Sirk
Screenplay............Peg Fenwick
Story.................Edna Lee
                          and Harry Lee

Cast:

Cary Scott.............Jane Wyman
Ron Kirby..............ROCK HUDSON
Sara Warren...........Agnes Moorehead
Harvey................Conrad Nagel
Kay Scott.............Gloria Talbott
Ned...................William Reynolds
Alida Anderson........Virginia Grey
Mick Anderson.........Charles Drake
Dr. Hennessy..........Hayden Rorke
Mona Plash............Jacqueline de Wit

(31) **Never Say Goodbye**
Universal (1956) color/96 minutes
Producer..............Albert J. Cohen
Director..............Jerry Hopper
Uncredited director.....Douglas Sirk
Screenplay............Charles Hoffman
    —based on the play *Come Prima, Meglio di Prima* by Luigi Pirandello;
      and a screenplay by Bruce Manning, John Klorer, and Leonard Lee

Cast:

Dr. Michael Parker	ROCK HUDSON
Lisa Gosting (Dorian Kent)	Cornell Borchers
Victor	George Sanders
Dr. Bailey	Ray Collins
Dave Heller.............	David Janssen
Suzy Parker.............	Shelley Fabares
Miss Tucker	Helen Wallace
Professor Zimmelman ...	John E. Wengraf
Dr. Kenneth Evans	Robert Simon
Dr. Kelly Andrews	Raymond Greenleaf

(32) Written on the Wind
Universal (1956) color/99 minutes
Producer .... Albert Zugsmith
Director .... Douglas Sirk
Screenplay............. George Zuckerman
—based on the novel *Written on the Wind* by
    Robert Wilder

Cast:

Mitch Wayne	ROCK HUDSON
Lucy Moore Hadley	Lauren Bacall
Kyle Hadley	Robert Stack
Marylee Hadley	Dorothy Malone
Jasper Hadley..........	Robert Keith
Biff Miley	Grant Williams
Dan Willis	Robert J. Wilke
Dr. Paul Cochrane	Edward C. Platt
Hoak Wayne...........	Harry Shannon
Roy Carter	John Larch

(33) Giant*
Warner Brothers (1956) color/198 minutes
Producers .... George Stevens
                and Henry Ginsberg
Director .... George Stevens
Screenplay............. Fred Guiol
                and Ivan Moffat
—based on the novel *Giant* by Edna Ferber

---

available on videocassette

Cast:

Leslie Benedict	Elizabeth Taylor
Bick Benedict	ROCK HUDSON
Jett Rink	James Dean
Luz Benedict	Mercedes McCambridge
Uncle Bawley	Chill Wills
Vashti Snythe	Jane Withers
Pinky Snythe	Robert Nichols
Jordan Benedict III	Dennis Hopper
Juana	Elsa Cardenas
Judy Benedict	Fran Bennett
Luz Benedict II	Carroll Baker
Bob Dace	Earl Holliman
Dr. Horace Lynnton	Paul Fix
Lacey Lynnton	Carolyn Craig
Mrs. Horace Lynnton	Judith Evelyn
Sir David Karfrey	Rodney (Rod) Taylor
Old Polo	Alexander Scourby
Angel Obregon II	Sal Mineo

(34) **Four Girls in Town**
Universal (1956) color/85 minutes

Producer	Aaron Rosenberg
Director	Jach Sher
Screenplay	Jach Sher

Cast:

Mike Snowden	George Nader
Kathy Conway	Julia Adams
Ina Schiller	Marianne Cook
Maria Antonelli	Elsa Martinelli
Vicki Dauray	Gia Scala
Johnny Pryor	Sydney Chaplin
Spencer Farrington, Jr.	Grant Williams
Tom Grant	John Gavin
and	
as himself	ROCK HUDSON

(35) **Battle Hymn**
Universal (1957) color/108 minutes
Producer ....Ross Hunter
Director ....Douglas Sirk
Screenplay..............Charles Grayson
—based on the autobiography *Battle Hymn* by
Colonel Dean Hess

Cast:

Colonel Dean Hess ......ROCK HUDSON
Mary Hess ....Martha Hyer
Sergeant Herman ....Dan Duryea
Captain Skidmore ....Don De Fore
En Soon Yang ....Anna Kashfi
Major Moore ....Jock Mahoney
Deacon Edwards ....Carl Benton Reid
Lieutenant Maples.......James Edwards
General Kim ....Richard Loo
Mess Sergeant ....Alan Hale

(36) **Something of Value**
M-G-M (1957) black & white/113 minutes
Producer ....Pandro S. Berman
Director ....Richard Brooks
Screenplay..............Richard Brooks
—based on the novel *Something of Value* by Robert C. Ruark

Cast:

Peter McKenzie ....ROCK HUDSON
Holly Keith ....Dana Wynter
Elizabeth ....Wendy Hiller
Kimani ....Sidney Poitier
Njogu ....Juano Hernandez
Leader ....William Marshall
Jeff Newton ....Robert Beatty
Henry McKenzie ....Walter Fitzgerald
Joe Matson ....Michael Pate
Lathela ....Ivan Dixon

(37) The Tarnished Angels
Universal (1957) black & white/91 minutes
Producer . . . . Albert Zugsmith
Director . . . . Douglas Sirk
Screenplay . . . . George Zuckerman
—based on the novel *Pylon* by William Faulkner

Cast:

Burke Devlin . . . . ROCK HUDSON
Roger Shumann . . . . Robert Stack
LaVerne Shumann . . . . . . Dorothy Malone
Jiggs . . . . Jack Carson
Matt Ord . . . . Robert Middleton
Colonel Fineman . . . . Alan Reed
Sam Hagood . . . . Alexander Lockwood
Jack Shumann . . . . Chris Olsen
Hank . . . . Robert J. Wilke
Frank Burnham . . . . Troy Donahue

(38) A Farewell to Arms
Twentieth Century–Fox (1957) color/152 minutes
Producer . . . . David O. Selznick
Director . . . . Charles Vidor
Screenplay . . . . Ben Hecht
—based on the novel *A Farewell to Arms* by Ernest Hemingway

Cast:

Lieutenant Frederick
    Henry . . . . ROCK HUDSON
Nurse Catherine Barkley . Jennifer Jones
Major Alessandro Rinaldi Vittorio De Sica
Father Galli . . . . Alberto Sordi
Miss Van Campen . . . . . . Mercedes McCambridge
Dr. Emerich . . . . Oscar Homolka
Helen Ferguson . . . . Elaine Stritch
Passini . . . . Leopaldo Trieste
Aymo . . . . Franco Interlenghi
Captain Bassi . . . . Georges Brehat

(39) **Twilight for the Gods**
Universal (1958) color/199 minutes
Producer . . . . Gordon Kay
Director . . . . Joseph Pevney
Screenplay . . . . Ernest K. Gann
   —based on the novel *Twilight for the Gods* by
      Ernest K. Gann

Cast:

David Bell . . . . ROCK HUDSON
Charlotte King . . . . Cyd Charisse
First Mate Ramsay . . . . . . Arthur Kennedy
Harry Hutton . . . . Leif Erickson
Yancey . . . . Charles McGraw
Reverend Butterfield . . . . Ernest Truex
Oliver Wiggins . . . . Richard Haydn
Ethel Peacock . . . . Judith Evelyn
Old Brown . . . . Wallace Ford
Feodor Morris . . . . Vladimir Sololoff

(40) **This Earth Is Mine**
Universal (1959) color/123 minutes
Executive producer . . . . . . Edward Muhl
Producers . . . . Casey Robinson
                                    and Claude Heilman
Director . . . . Henry King
Screenplay . . . . Casey Robinson
   —based on the novel *The Cup and the Sword* by
      Alice Tisdale Hobart

Cast:

John Rambeau . . . . ROCK HUDSON
Elizabeth Rambeau . . . . . . Jean Simmons
Martha Fairon . . . . Dorothy McGuire
Philippe Rambeau . . . . Claude Rains
Francis Fairon . . . . Kent Smith
Charlotte Rambeau . . . . . . Anna Lee
Buz . . . . Cindy Robbins
Luigi . . . . Ken Scott
Andre Swann . . . . Francis Bethencourt
Monica . . . . Stacey Graham

(41) Pillow Talk*

Universal (1959) color/105 minutes

Producers	Ross Hunter and Martin Melcher
Director	Michael Gordon
Screenplay	Stanley Shapiro and Maurice Richlin
Story	Russell Rouse and Clarence Green

Cast:

Brad Allen	ROCK HUDSON
Jan Marrow	Doris Day
Jonathan Forbes	Tony Randall
Alma	Thelma Ritter
Pierot	Marcel Dalio
Tony Walters	Nick Adams
Marie	Julia Meade
Mrs. Walters	Lee Patrick
Dr. Maxwell	Alex Gerry
Nurse Resnick	Mary McCarthy
Nightclub entertainer	Perry Blackwell

(42) The Last Sunset

Universal (1961) color/112 minutes

Producers	Eugene Frenke and Edward Lewis
Director	Robert Aldrich
Screenplay	Dalton Trumbo

—based on the novel *Sundown at Crazy Horse* by Howard Rigsby

Cast:

Dana Stribling	ROCK HUDSON
Brendan O'Malley	Kirk Douglas
Belle Breckenridge	Dorothy Malone
John Breckenridge	Joseph Cotton
Missy Breckenridge	Carole Lynley
Frank Hobbs	Neville Brand

---

*available on videocassette

Milton Wing . . . . Regis Toomey
Julesberg Kid . . . . Rad Fulton
Bowman . . . . Adam Williams
Ed Hobbs . . . . Jack Elam

(43) **Come September**
Universal (1961) color/112 minutes
Producer . . . . Robert Arthur
Associate producer . . . . . . Henry Willson
Director . . . . Robert Mulligan
Screenplay . . . . Stanley Shapiro

Cast:

Robert Talbot . . . . ROCK HUDSON
Lisa Fellini . . . . Gina Lollobrigida
Sandy Stevens . . . . Sandra Dee
Tony . . . . Bobby Darin
Maurice Clevall . . . . Walter Slezak
Margaret . . . . Brenda De Banzie
Anna . . . . Rosanna Rory
Spencer . . . . Ronald Howard
Beagle . . . . Joel Grey
Sparrow . . . . Ronnie Haran

(44) **Lover Come Back**
Universal (1961) color/107 minutes
Executive producer . . . . . . Robert Arthur
Producers . . . . Stanley Shapiro
                                      and Martin Melcher
Director . . . . Delbert Mann
Screenplay . . . . Stanley Shapiro
                                      and Paul Henning

Cast:

Jerry Webster . . . . ROCK HUDSON
Carol Templeton . . . . Doris Day
Peter Ramsey . . . . Tony Randall
Rebel Davis . . . . Edie Adams
J. Paxton Miller . . . . Jack Oakie
Dr. Linus Tyler . . . . Jack Kruschen
Millie . . . . Ann B. Davis
Hadley . . . . Joe Flynn

Brackett ....Howard St. John
Elevator Operator ....Ted Bessell

(45) **The Spiral Road**
Universal (1962) color/145 minutes
Producer ....Robert Arthur
Director ....Robert Mulligan
Screenplay.............John Lee Mahin
and Neil Paterson
—based on the novel *The Spiral Road* by Jan De Hartog

Cast:

Dr. Anton Drager ....ROCK HUDSON
Dr. Brits Jansen ....Burl Ives
Els ....Gena Rowlands
William Wattereus.......Geoffrey Keen
Louise Kramer ....Neva Patterson
Dr. Sordjano ....Will Kuluva
Frolick ....Philip Abbott
Dr. Kramer ....Larry Gates
Inspector Bevers ....Karl Swenson
The Sultan ....Edgar Stehli

(46) **A Gathering of Eagles**
Universal (1963) color/116 minutes
Producer ....Sy Bartlett
Director ....Delbert Mann
Screenplay.............Robert Pirosh
Story ....Sy Bartlett

Cast:

Jim Caldwell ....ROCK HUDSON
Hollis Farr.............Rod Taylor
Victoria Caldwell ....Mary Peach
Colonel Fowler ....Barry Sullivan
General Kirby..........Kevin McCarthy
Colonel Garcia ....Henry Silva
Mrs. Fowler............Leora Dama
Sergeant Banning ....Robert Lansing
General Hewitt..........Leif Erickson
Colonel Josten ....Richard Anderson

(47) **Marilyn**
Twentieth Century–Fox (1963) color and black
& white/83 minutes
Commentary . . . . Harold Medford
Editor . . . . Pepe Torres

Cast:

As herself in filmclips . . . . Marilyn Monroe
Narrator . . . . ROCK HUDSON

(48) **Man's Favorite Sport?**
Universal (1964) color/120 minutes
Producer . . . . Howard Hawks
Associate Producer . . . . . . Paul Helmick
Director . . . . Howard Hawks
Screenplay . . . . John Fenton Murray
   —based on the story "The Girl Who Almost
   Got Away" by Pat Frank

Cast:

Roger Willoughby . . . . ROCK HUDSON
Abigail Page . . . . Paula Prentiss
Isolde "Easy" Mueller . . . . Maria Perschy
Tex Connors . . . . Charlene Holt
William Cadwalader . . . . . John McGiver
Major Phipps . . . . Roscoe Karns
Skaggs . . . . Forrest Lewis
Bagley . . . . Regis Toomey
John Screaming Eagle . . . Norman Alden
Tom . . . . Don Allen

(49) **Send Me No Flowers**
Universal (1964) color/100 minutes
Executive producer . . . . . . Martin Melcher
Producer . . . . Harry Keller
Director . . . . Norman Jewison
Screenplay . . . . Julius Epstein
   —based on the play *Send Me No Flowers* by
   Norman Barasch

Cast:

George Kimball	ROCK HUDSON
Judy Kimball	Doris Day
Arnold Nash	Tony Randall
Bert Power	Clint Walker
Dr. Ralph Morrisey	Edward Andrews
Linda Mullard	Patricia Parry
Winston Burr	Hal March
Mr. Akins	Paul Lynde
Vito	Clive Clerk
Milkman	Dave Willock

(50) **Strange Bedfellows**
Universal (1964) color/99 minutes
Producer	Melvin Frank
Associate producer	Hal C. Kern
Director	Melvin Frank
Screenplay	Melvin Frank
Story	Norman Panama and Melvin Frank

Cast:

Carter Harrison	ROCK HUDSON
Toni Vincente	Gina Lollobrigida
Richard Bramwell	Gig Young
Harry Jones	Edward Judd
Assistant Mortician	Terry-Thomas
Carter's Taxi Driver	Arthur Haynes
J.L. Stevens	Howard St. John
Aggressive Woman	Nancy Kulp
Toni's Taxi Driver	David King
Mavis	Peggy Rea

(51) **A Very Special Favor**
Universal (1965) color/104 minutes
Executive producer	Robert Arthur
Producer	Stanley Shapiro
Director	Michael Gordon
Screenplay	Stanley Shapiro

Cast:

Paul.....................ROCK HUDSON
Lauren ....Leslie Caron
Michel ....Charles Boyer
Etienne.................Walter Slezak
Arnold ....Dick Shawn
Harry ....Larry Storch
Mickey ....Nita Talbot
Mother Plum ....Norma Varden
Pete.....................George Furth
Claude ....Marcel Hillaire

(52) **Blindfold**
Universal (1966) color/102 minutes
Executive producer......Robert Arthur
Producer ....Marvin Schwartz
Director ....Philip Dunne
Screenplay..............Philip Dunne
                              and W. H. Menger
   —based on the novel *Blindfold* by Lucille Fletcher

Cast:

Dr. Bartholomew Snow ..ROCK HUDSON
Victoria Vail ....Claudia Carindale
Fitzpatrick ....Dean Stockwell
General Prat ....Jack Warden
Harrigan ....Brad Dexter
Smitty ....Anne Seymour
Arthur Vincenti ....Alejandro Rey
Captain Davis ....Hari Rhodes
Michelangelo Vincenti ...Vito Scotti
Angela Clarke ....Lavinia Vincenti

(53) **Seconds**
Paramount (1966) black & white/106 minutes
Producer ....Edward Lewis
Director ....John Frankenheimer
Screenplay..............Lewis John Carlino
   —based on the novel *Seconds* by David Ely

Cast:

Antiochus Wilson ....ROCK HUDSON
Nora Marcus...........Salome Jens
Authur Hamilton ....John Randolph
The Old Man ....Will Geer
Mr. Ruby ....Jeff Corey
Dr. Innes ....Richard Anderson
Charlie Evans ....Murry Hamilton
Dr. Morris ....Karl Swenson
Davalo ....Khigh Dhiegh
Emily Hamilton ....Frances Reid

(54) **Tobruk**
Universal (1966) color/110 minutes
Producer ....Gene Corman
Director ....Arthur Hiller
Screenplay.............Leo V. Gordon

Cast:

Major Donald Craig .....ROCK HUDSON
Captain Kurt Bergman ..George Peppard
Colonel John Harker ....Nigel Green
Lieutenant Max
    Mohnfeld..........Guy Stockwell
Sergeant-Major Tyne ....Jack Weston
Alfie ....Norman Rossington
Dolan ....Percy Herbert
Henry Portman ....Liam Redmond
Cheryl Portman ....Heidy Hunt
Sergeant Krug ....Leo Gordon

(55) **Ice Station Zebra***
M-G-M (1968) color/152 minutes
Producer ....Martin Ransohoff
Associate producer ......James C. Pratt
Director ....John Sturges
Screenplay.............Douglas Heyes
Screen story ....Harry Julian
    —based on the novel *Ice Station Zebra* by Alistair
    MacLean

---

*available on videocassette

Cast:

Commander Fames
     Ferraday . . . . .ROCK HUDSON
Boris Vaslov . . . . .Ernest Borgnine
David Jones. . . . . .Patrick McGoohan
Captain Leslie Anders . . .Jim Brown
Lieutenant Russell
     Walker . . . . .Tony Bill
Admiral Garvey . . . . .Lloyd Nolan
Colonel Ostrovsky . . . . . .Alf Kjellin
Lieutenant Commander
     Raebum . . . . .Gerald S. O'Loughlin
Lieutenant Jonathan
     Hansen. . . . . .Ted Hartley
Lieutenant George Mills .Murray Rose

(56) **A Fine Pair**
(*Ruba Al Promissmo Tuo*)
National General (1969) color/115 minutes
Executive producer . . . . . .Franco Cristaldi
Producer . . . . .Leo L. Fuchs
Director . . . . .Francesco Maselli
Screenplay . . . . .Francesco Maselli
                   and Luisa Montagnana
Story . . . . .Luisa Montagnana

Cast:

Captain Mike Harmon . . .ROCK HUDSON
Esmeralda Marini . . . . . . .Claudia Cardinale
Roger . . . . .Thomas Milian
Chief Wellman . . . . .Leon Askin
Mrs. Walker . . . . .Ellen Corby
Franz . . . . .Walter Giller
Uncle Camillo. . . . . .Guido Alberti
Albert Kinsky . . . . .Peter Dane

(57) **The Undefeated***
Twentieth Century–Fox (1969) color/118 minutes
Producer . . . . .Robert Jacks
Director . . . . .Andrew V. McLaglen

---

*available on videocassette

Screenplay . . . . James Lee Barrett
Story . . . . Stanley L. Hough

Cast:

Colonel John Henry
　　　Thomas . . . . John Wayne
Colonel James Langdon . . ROCK HUDSON
General Rojas . . . . Tony Aguilar
Blue Boy . . . . Roman Gabriel
Ann Langdon . . . . Marian McCargo
Margaret Langdon . . . . . Lee Meriwether
Little George . . . . Merlin Olsen
Charlotte Langdon . . . . . Melissa Newman
Jeff Newby . . . . Bruce Cabot
Bubba Wilkes . . . . (Jan) Michael Vincent
Short Grub . . . . Ben Johnson
Major Sanders . . . . Royal Dano
Dan Norse . . . . Richard Mulligan
Christian . . . . John Agar

(58) **Darling Lili**
Paramount (1970) color/136 minutes
Executive producer . . . . . . Owen Crump
Associate producer . . . . . Ken Wales
Director . . . . Blake Edwards
Screenplay . . . . Blake Edwards
　　　　　　　　　and William Peter Blatty

Cast:

Lili Smith . . . . Julie Andrews
Major William Larrabee . . ROCK HUDSON
Kurt von Ruger . . . . Jeremy Kemp
T.C. . . . . Lance Percival
Youngblood Carson . . . . Michael Witney
Major Duvalle . . . . Jacques Marin
Lieutenant Liggett . . . . Andre Maranne
Crepe Suzette . . . . Gloria Paul
Bedford . . . . Bernard Kay
Emma . . . . Doreen Koegh

(59) **Hornet's Nest**
United Artists (1970) color/109 minutes
Producer ....Stanley S. Canter
Director ....Phil Karlson
Screenplay..............S. S. Schweitzer
Story...................S. S. Schweitzer
                                    and Stanley Colbert

Cast:

Captain Turner ....ROCK HUDSON
Bianca ....Sylva Koscina
Aldo ....Mark Colleano
von Hecht ....Sergio Fantoni
Major Taussig ....Jacques Sernas
Schwalberg ....Giacomo Rossi Stuart
Carlo...................Mauro Gravini
Dino ....John Fordyce
Tekko..................Daniel Keller
Giorgio.................Daniel Dempsey

(60) **Pretty Maids All in a Row**
MGM (1971) color/92 minutes
Producer ....Gene Roddenberry
Director ....Roger Vadim
Screenplay.............Gene Roddenberry
    —based on the novel *Pretty Maids All in a Row*
    by Francis Pollini

Cast:

Michael "Tiger" McDrew.ROCK HUDSON
Miss Smith..............Angie Dickinson
Captain Sam Surcher ....Telly Savalas
Donce de Leon Harper ..John David Carson
Proffer ....Roddy McDowell
Chief John Poldaski .....Keenan Wynn
Follo ....James Doohan
Grady ....William Campbell
Miss Harriet Craymire ...Susan Tolsky
Jean McDrew ....Barbara Leigh

(61) **Showdown**
Universal (1973) color/99 minutes
Producer .... George Seaton
Associate producer ...... Donald Roberts
Director .... George Seaton
Screenplay............. Theodore Taylor
Story .... Hank Fine

Cast:

Chuck Jarvis .... ROCK HUDSON
Billy Massey .... Dean Martin
Kate Jarvis............. Susan Clark
Art Williams .... Donald Moffat
P. J. Wilson .... John McLiam
Martinez .... Charles Baca
Clem .... Jackson Kane
Perry Williams .... Ben Zeller
Earl Cole .... John Richard Gill
Pook .... Ed Begley, Jr.

(62) **Embryo***
Cine Artists (1976) color/108 minutes
Executive producer ..... Sandy Howard
Producers .... Arnold H. Orgolini
                            and Anita Doohan
Director .... Ralph Nelson
Screenplay............. Anita Doohan
Story .... Jack W. Thomas

Cast:

Dr. Paul Holliston ...... ROCK HUDSON
Martha .... Diane Ladd
Victoria .... Barbara Carrera
Riley .... Roddy McDowall
Helen .... Ann Schedeen
Gordon .... John Elrick
Dr. Wiston............. Jack Colvin
Collier .... Vincent Bagetta
Trainer .... Joyce Spitz
as herself .... Dr. Joyce Brothers

---

*available on videocassette

(63) **Avalanche***
New World Pictures (1978) color/91 minutes
Executive Producer......Paul Rapp
Producer ....Rogert Corman
Director ....Corey Allen
Screenplay.............Claude Pola
                              and Corey Allen
Story ....Frances Doel

Cast:

David Shelby............ROCK HUDSON
Caroline Bruce Shelby ...Mia Farrow
Nick Thorne............Robert Forster
Florence Shelby ....Jeanette Nolan
Bruce Scott ....Rick Moses
Mark Elliot ....Barry Primus
Henry McDede ....Steve Franken
Tina Elliot ....Cathey Paine
Phil Prentiss ....Jerry Douglas
Leo the Coach ....Tony Carbone

(64) **The Mirror Crack'd***
EMI Films Ltd. (1980) color/105 minutes
Producers ....John Brabourne
                              and Richard Goodwin
Director ....Guy Hamilton
Screenplay.............Jonathan Hales
                              and Barry Sandler
—based on the novel *The Mirror Crack'd* by
   Agatha Christie

Cast:

Miss Marple ....Angela Lansbury
Marina Gregg (Rudd)....Elizabeth Taylor
Jason Rudd.............ROCK HUDSON
Lola Brewster ....Kim Novak
Marty N. Fenn ....Tony Curtis
Inspector Craddock .....Edward Fox
Ella Zielinsky ....Geraldine Chaplin
Cherry ....Wendy Morgan

---

*available on videocassette

Bates . . . . Charles Gray
Heather Babcock . . . . Maureen Bennett

(65) **The Ambassador**
Cannon Films (1984) color/95 minutes
Producers . . . . Menaham Golan
and Yoram Globus
Director . . . . J. Lee Thompson
Screenplay . . . . Max Jack

Cast:

Hacker . . . . Robert Mitchum
Alex . . . . Ellen Burstyn
Stevenson . . . . ROCK HUDSON
Hashimi . . . . Fabio Testi
Eretz . . . . Donald Pleasence
Rachel . . . . Heli Goldenberg
Tova . . . . Michael Bat-Adam
Abe . . . . Ori Levy
Assad . . . . Uri Gavriel
Ze'ev . . . . Zachi Nov

TELEVISION:

Movies & Mini-Series:

(1) **Once Upon a Dead Man**
Made-for-TV Movie
NBC-TV (1971) color/95 minutes
Executive producer......Leonard B. Stern
Producer ....Paul Mason
Director ....Leonard B. Stern
Teleplay................Leonard B. Stern
and Chester Krumholz

Cast:

Stewart McMillan........ROCK HUDSON
Sally MacMillan ....Susan St. James
Sergeant Enright ....John Schuck
Chief Andy Yeakel .....Jack Albertson
André Stryker ....René Auberjonois
Edmond Corday ....Kurt Kasznar
Wortzel ....Jonathan Harris
Gregory Constantine ....Herb Edelman
John Patterson ....James Wainwright
Dr. Hinton ....Stacy Keach, Sr.

(2) **Wheels**
Mini-Series
NBC-TV (1978) color/five-part series

Cast:

Adam Trenton..........ROCK HUDSON
Erica Trenton..........Lee Remick

Greg Trenton	Howard McGillin
Kirk Trenton	James Carroll Jordan
Hub Hewitson	Tim O'Connor
Rusty Horton	Gerald S. O'Laughlin
Rollie Knight	Harold Sylvester
Teresa Chapman	Adele Mara
Lowell Baxter	Ralph Bellamy
Jody Horton	Lisa Eilbacher
Smokey Stephenson	Tony Franciosa
Barbara Lipton	Blair Brown
Leonard Wingate	Fred Williamson
Ursula	Jessica Walter
Newkirk	Al White

(3) **The Martian Chronicles***
Mini-Series
Charles Fries Productions (1979) color/three-part series:

   Part One: "The Expeditions" 120 minutes*
   Part Two: "The Settlers" 97 minutes*
   Part Three: "The Martians" 97 minutes*

Executive producers	Charles Fries and Dick Berg
Producers	Andrew Donally and Milton Subotsky
Director	Michael Anderson
Teleplay	Richard Matheson

   —based on the novel *The Martian Chronicles* by Ray Bradbury

Cast:

Colonel John Wilder	ROCK HUDSON
Captain Jeff Sender	Bernie Casey
Ben Driscoll	Christopher Connelly
Arthur Black	Nicholas Hammond
Father Stone	Roddy McDowall
Captain Sam Parkhill	Darren McGavin
Genevieve	Bernadette Peters
Anna Lustig	Maria Schell
Elma Parkhill	Joyce Van Patten

---

*available on videocassette

Father Peregrine ....Fritz Weaver
Ruth Wilder ....Gayle Hunnicutt

(4) **The Starmaker**
Mini-Series
(1981) color/200 minutes
Director ....Lou Antonio
Writer.................William Bast

Cast:

ROCK HUDSON
Suzanne Pleshette
Melanie Griffith
Teri Copley
April Clough
Cathie Shirriff
Brenda Vaccaro
Ed McMahon
Titos Vandis

(5) **World War III**
Mini-Series in two parts
Telepictures Corporation (1982) color/200 minutes
Executive producers .....Pat Finnegan
                           and Bill Finnegan
Producer ....Bruce Lansbury
Director ....David Greene
Teleplay...............Robert L. Joseph

Cast:

Col. Jacob Caffey........David Soul
Secretary Gorny.........Brian Keith
Kate Breckenridge ......Cathy Lee Crosby
Dorothy Longworth .....Katherine Helmond
                and
President McKenna......ROCK HUDSON

(6) **The Vegas Strip War**
ITC Entertainment (1984)

Cast:

ROCK HUDSON
James Earl Jones
Sharon Stone

TV Series:

(1) **McMillan and Wife**
NBC-TV (1971–1976)
McMillan
NBC-TV (1976–1977)

Cast:

Commissioner Stewart
    McMillan .... ROCK HUDSON
Sally McMillan
    (1971–1976) .... Susan Saint James
Sergeant Charles Enright John Schuck
Mildred (1971–1976) .... Nancy Walker
Agatha (1976–1977) .... Martha Raye
Sergeant Steve DiMaggio
    (1976–1977) .... Richard Gilliland
Maggie (1976–1977) ..... Gloria Strook

(2) **The Devlin Connection**
NBC-TV (1982)

Cast:

Brian Devlin .... ROCK HUDSON
Nick Corsello .... Jack Scalia
Lauren Dane .... Leigh Taylor Young
Lieutenant Earl Bordon.. Louis Giambalvo
Mrs. Watanabe .... Takayo

(3) **Dynasty**
ABC-TV (1984–1985) Aaron Spelling Productions
Producers .... Camille Marchetta
                     and Edward De Blasio

Creators . . . . Richard Shapiro
                                    and Esther Shapiro
Teleplay . . . . Edward De Blasio
Story . . . . Camille Marchetta
Director . . . . various

Cast:

Blake Carrington . . . . John Forsythe
Krystle Carrington . . . . . Linda Evans
Jeff Colby . . . . John James
Claudia Carrington . . . . . Pamela Bellwood
Adam Carrington . . . . Gordon Thompson
Steven Carrington . . . . . . Jack Coleman
Dex Dexter . . . . Michael Nader
Amanda Carrington . . . . . Catherine Oxenberg
Prince Michael . . . . Michael Praed
Dominique Deveraux . . . . Diahann Carroll
Sammy Jo Reece . . . . Heather Locklear
               Special Guest Stars
Lady Ashley . . . . Ali McGraw
Daniel Reece . . . . ROCK HUDSON
                   and
Alexis . . . . Joan Collins

Guest Appearances on TV Shows:

(1) **This Is Your Life**
     (December 17, 1952)

(2) **The Jack Benny Show**
     (1954)
         —with Hugh Downs, and Dennis Day

(3) **I Love Lucy**
     (1955)

(4) **The 30th Annual Academy Awards**
     (March 26, 1958)
         —with Mae West, singing "Baby, It's Cold
         Outside"

(5) **The Big Party**
(October 8, 1959)
—with Esther Williams, Tallulah Bankhead, and
Sammy Davis Jr.

(6) **The Carol Burnett Show**
(1966)

(7) **The Kraft Music Hall**
"The Hollywood Musicals"
(September 20, 1967)
—with Connie Stevens, Michelle Lee, and Bobby
Van

(8) **Dinah Shore's Christmas Special**
(December, 1975)

—plus, various TV talk shows

THEATER

(1) **I Do! I Do!**
(1973) The Huntington Hartford Theater
Los Angeles, California
ROCK HUDSON with Carol Burnett

(2) **I Do! I Do!**
(Summer 1974) tour including Dallas, Texas; St.
Louis, Missouri; and Washington, D.C.
ROCK HUDSON with Carol Burnett

(3) **I Do! I Do!**
(February 1976) London, England
ROCK HUDSON with Juliet Prowse

(4) **John Brown's Body**
(Spring and Summer 1976) 20 city American tour
ROCK HUDSON with Claire Trevor, Leif
Erickson, and the Voices of Young America

(5) **Camelot**
(Summer 1977) American tour
ROCK HUDSON

(6) **On the Twentieth Century**
(1979) American tour including Detroit, Michigan,
and Chicago, Illinois
ROCK HUDSON with Judy Kaye and Imogene
Coca

DISCOGRAPHY:

Singles:
(1) **"Pillow Talk"** (side one) Decca Records (1959)
    "Roly Poly" (side two)

Albums:
(1) **Rock, Gently**
    Album (ROCK HUDSON sings the songs of Rod
    McKuen)
    Stanyon Records (SR 10014) (1970)
    Producer . . . . Rod McKuen
    Musical director . . . . Rod McKuen
    Conductor . . . . Arthur Greenslade
    Vocals . . . . ROCK HUDSON
      Side One:
        "Open the Window and See All the Clowns"
          (Rod McKuen) 2:28
        "I'll Say Goodbye"
          (McKuen/Becaud) 2:54
        "I've Been to Town"
          (Rod McKuen) 2:24
        "Things Bright and Beautiful"
          (Clark/McKuen/Grant) 2:55
        "As I Love My Own"
          (Rod McKuen) 2:55
        "Gone with the Cowboys"
          (Rod McKuen) 3:10
        "Love's Been Good to Me"
          (Rod McKuen) 3:15
      Side Two:
        "Meantime"
          (Rod McKuen) 2:38

187

"You Pass Me By"
    (Rod McKuen) 2:04
"So Long, Stay Well"
    (Rod McKuen) 1:33
"Blessings in Shades of Green"
    (Rod McKuen) 3:00
"Happy Birthday to Me"
    (Rod McKuen) 2:26
"Jean" (Theme from *The Prime of Miss
    Jean Brodie*)
    (Rod McKuen) 3:00
"Lonesome Cities"
    (Rod McKuen) 2:45

BIBLIOGRAPHY

—*The All-Americans* by James Robert Parish and Don E. Stanke. Rainbow Books; Carlstadt, New Jersey (1978)

—*Doris Day* by George Morris. Pyramid Books; New York, New York (1976)

—*Doris Day, Her Own Story* by A.E. Hotchner. William Morrow; New York, New York (1975)

—*Elizabeth Taylor, The Last Star* by Kitty Kelley. Dell; New York, New York (1982)

—*Monty, A Biography of Montgomery Clift* by Robert LaGuardia. Avon Books; New York, New York (1978)

—*Movies on TV* by Steven H. Schueuer. Bantam Books; New York, New York (1985 Edition)

—*TV Movies 1985–86* edited by Leonard Maltin. Signet Books; New York, New York (1984 Edition)